’s

Guide to the

Internet

The BOOK LOVER'S *guide to the* INTERNET

EVAN MORRIS

REVISED AND UPDATED

Fawcett Columbine
The Ballantine Publishing Group • New York

A Fawcett Columbine Book
Published by The Ballantine Publishing Group

 Published in the United States by The Ballantine Publishing Group, a division of Random House, Inc., New York, and simultaneously in Canada by Random House of Canada Limited, Toronto. This is the revised edition of a work originally published by The Ballantine Publishing Group in 1996.

http://www.randomhouse.com

Library of Congress Catalog Card Number: 98-96166

ISBN: 0-449-00227-6

Cover design by Cathy Colbert
Cover photograph courtesy of Tony Stone Images

Manufactured in the United States of America

First Ballantine Books Edition: June 1996
Revised Ballantine Books Edition: July 1998

10 9 8 7 6 5 4 3 2 1

For Kathy, with all my love.

Thanks to my wife, Kathy, who first encouraged me to write this book and was rewarded by being stuck with editing and proofreading the manuscript; to my siblings, for their encouragement; to my agent, Nancy Yost of Lowenstein Associates, for her good judgment and persistence; to my editor at Random House, Phebe Kirkham, for her awesome ability to coax order out of chaos; to Danny Choriki and Dan Poor, for their invaluable technical assistance; to the staffs of Interport, Bway and The WELL, and to all my friends, for their humor and support.

Contents

Preface to the Second Edition xiii

Chapter 1 WHAT IS THE INTERNET, WHERE DID IT COME FROM, WHERE IS IT GOING, AND DO I GET TO KEEP MY BOOKS WHEN WE GET THERE? 1

- What Is the Internet, Anyway? 2
- A Very Brief History of the Net 4
- But What Does All This Have to Do With Books and Reading? 6
- Book Lovers on the Net 8
- The Culture of the Net 12
  - A Few Principles of Netiquette 14
  - What's Mine Is Ours 14
  - Growing Pains 15
- Books, the Net, and the Future of Reading 18

Chapter 2 HOOKING UP: SIMPLE WAYS TO CONNECT YOURSELF TO THE INTERNET 21

- Equipment 23
  - Computers 23
  - Software 26
  - Modems 27
  - Telephone Lines 29
- Internet Access Without a Computer 30
- Gateways to the Internet: How to Pick a Service Provider 32

Free (or Nearly Free) Access to the Net 32
Commercial Internet Services 34
Note to Parents 40
Independent Internet Service Providers 43
Specialty Providers for Readers and Book Lovers 46

Chapter 3 GETTING THERE FROM HERE: THE MANY PATHS THROUGH THE INTERNET 51

The World Wide Web and Its Search Engines 52
Search Engines 56
The Web and Book Lovers 58
The Web Marches On 60
FTP 62
Telnet 65
IRC (Internet Relay Chat) 66

Chapter 4 USENET DISCUSSION GROUPS AND WEB FORUMS: ADDING YOUR TWO CENTS' WORTH 69

Usenet Newsgroups 71
The Organization of Usenet Newsgroups 74
Usenet Newsreaders 78
Usenet Newsgroups of Particular Interest to Readers 81
Finding Information on Usenet 86
Starting a Usenet Newsgroup 87
The Downside of Usenet 90
Web-Based Conferencing Systems and Discussion Groups 91

Chapter 5 MAILING LISTS: NEWS AND VIEWS IN YOUR E-MAILBOX 95

Subscribing to a Mailing List 98
Finding a List to Join 99
Participating in a Mailing List 102
Mailing Lists and Your Sanity 103

Chapter 6 HOW TO BE YOUR OWN PUBLISHER: PUTTING YOURSELF ON-LINE 105

Posting Your Work on Usenet 106
Electronic Literary Journals and E-zines 107
Starting Your Own Electronic Newsletter 108
Publishing Yourself on the World Wide Web 111
What's Behind That Web Page? 112
Learning HTML 113
Web Page Construction Tools 114
Putting Your Page On-line 117
Points to Ponder About Your Web Page 117

Chapter 7 ON-LINE RESOURCES FOR BOOK LOVERS 120

Understanding Names and Places on the Internet 123
If You Have Problems With an Internet Address 125
Internet Metapages, Indexes, and Search Engines 126
General Indexes and Metapages 126
Search Engines 127
Indexes of Resources for Book Lovers 129
Frequently Asked Questions (FAQ) Files 132

Books and Authors 146
Authors 146
Children's Books and Reading Resources 165
Cultural Studies and Multicultural Literature 168
Gay, Lesbian, and Bisexual Literature 170
Humor 171
Mystery Literature 173
Poetry Resources 175
Romance Writing 179
Scholarly Literary Resources 180
Mythology and Folklore 181
Ancient and Classical Literature 183
Medieval Literature 184
Renaissance Literature 185
18th-Century and Romantic Literature 186
Victorian Literature 186
Modern Literature 187
Science Fiction, Fantasy, and Horror 188
Science Fiction and Fantasy Resources 188
Horror Fiction Resources 190
Resources for Horror, Science Fiction, and Fantasy Writers 190
Theater Resources 192
Women's Literary Resources 194
E-texts:
Books On-line 197
Commercial E-text Publishers and Distributors 201
Hypertext Literature 202
Bookstores and Publishers 203
Bookstores 203

Publishers 208
E-zines, Magazines, and Newspapers 210
Book Reviews 210
E-zines and Literary Journals 213
Magazines 228
Newspapers and Other News Sources 233
Indexes of Newspapers 233
Newspapers 234
Other Sources of News 238
Libraries and Reference Sources 240
Dictionaries and Other Language Resources 240
Dictionaries 240
Other General Language Resources 241
Libraries On-line 245
Reference Sources 248
Information About the U.S. Government 250
Other Helpful Reference Resources 251
Writing Resources 253
General Writing Resources 254
University Writing Programs and Writing Laboratories 256
Journalism Resources 256
Helpful Resources for Writers 257
Writers' Organizations 259
Screenwriting 259
Children's Writing Resources 260
Diaries and Collective Writing Projects 260
Sources of Information About the Internet 262

Chapter 8 KEEPING UP WITH THE NET: HOW TO STAY ABREAST OF NEW RESOURCES ON THE INTERNET 265

On-line Newsletters 266
Usenet Newsgroups 268
The Web 268
Magazines 269
Books 270

INDEX 273

ABOUT THE AUTHOR 285

Preface to the Second Edition

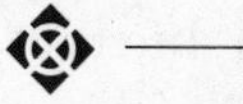

Second editions of books are usually occasions for fine-tuning the structure, polishing the prose, correcting a few inevitable typographical errors, and filling in whatever minor gaps have become apparent since the first edition was published.

In the case of *The Book Lover's Guide to the Internet*, however, putting together a second edition has meant compiling an almost entirely new book. The answers to almost every question the first edition covered, from "How can I get hooked up to the Internet without being a computer whiz?" to "What will I find when I get there?" to "How can I put my own writing on-line?" have changed, in many cases dramatically.

The culprit, of course, is the Internet itself, which stubbornly refuses to stop growing and changing. In the two years since the first edition of this book was published, both the Internet and the number of people using it on a regular basis have grown at an exponential rate. In the early 1990s, veteran Internet users started to speak of "Internet years." Like the "dog years" used to reckon Fido's age in human terms, Internet years were an attempt to keep tabs on the exploding popularity and rapid-fire technological development of the Net. Over the last two years, Internet years have been reckoned in mere months, as the Net itself has doubled again and again in size, depth, and technical sophistication to accommodate the tidal wave of new users logging on.

Today, more than 50 million people around the world are connected to the Internet. In 1994, the entire World Wide Web consisted of about 140 Web sites. Today there are more than 500,000 places to visit on the Web and literally thousands being added every day, many incorporating innovations such as streaming video and real-time chat facilities that would have seemed hopelessly futuristic only a few years ago.

But perhaps more important than the growth and development of the Net itself has been the "mainstreaming" of the Internet as a new dimension of everyday life for millions of people. When the first edition of this book was published, the Net was still something of a novelty. Almost everyone had a younger sister or a nephew who was "on the Net," but the Internet was viewed by the average citizen as a new and strange land, mysterious and possibly more than just a little menacing.

Today, millions of teachers, students, housewives, retirees, bus drivers, artists, lawyers, taxidermists, doctors, plumbers, and poets log on to the Net every day without giving it a second thought. Once there, they exchange e-mail, meet their friends in chat rooms and on bulletin boards, catch up on the latest news about their hobbies, research their family trees, buy everything from books to pet fish on-line, or just poke around the Net discovering something new with every mouse click. According to consumer surveys, the urge to "get on the Net" is now the primary reason buyers give for purchasing their first computer. Improvements in computer software have made it much easier to get "wired" to the Net, and faster modems have made traveling the Internet a far more enjoyable experience than it once was. The advent of such inventions as WebTV, which allows anyone who owns a TV to "surf the Net" without a computer, heralds the dawn of a new age in the relationship between the average, non-technical consumer and the Internet. The Internet is on the verge of becoming as commonplace a medium for communication, education, and entertainment as television or radio.

The premise of the first edition of this book—that the Internet represents a wonderful resource for anyone who is devoted to books and reading—has turned out to be an understatement. The Internet has added a whole new dimension to the experience of being a reader or writer. It has become, in fact, increasingly difficult to remain truly up-to-date with the world of books, literature, and the mass media without being hooked up to the Net.

Discussion groups and on-line forums devoted to books, whether organized around a particular author or covering an entire genre, have blossomed in every corner of the Net, from freestanding Web sites created by inspired fans to bulletin boards sponsored by such heavy hitters of the literary arena as *The New York Times Book Review* and *The Washington Post Book World.* Electronic magazines (e-zines) devoted to literature, already one of the fastest-growing segments of the Net when the first edition of this book was published, have managed to retain their youthful exuberance while developing a stable audience of devoted readers and writers. E-zines are indeed here to stay, as are their high-profile siblings, the on-line journals of literature, culture, politics, and the arts such as *Salon* and *Feed. Salon* in particular has made its mark with daily updates and such innovative features as on-line discussion groups on works of classic literature led by contemporary authors.

The Internet has also matured and expanded as a vital source of news for an increasing number of people worldwide. More than 3,000 newspapers, ranging from major metropolitan dailies to modest small-town journals, now have Web sites. Many of these sites also offer direct access to wire service news reports, allowing readers to follow news around the world in "real time" with constant updates. Hybrid TV-Web news sites, such as MSNBC and CBS's *Up to the Minute News,* offer TV viewers the background information their on-air broadcasts don't have time to present, and even the stodgy old BBC has made its World Service radio reports available on the Web, no shortwave radio required.

Nearly every major print magazine, from *The Atlantic Monthly* to *Reader's Digest,* now makes at least part of its content available on the Web. Publishers have discovered the Web as the perfect showcase for their products and most now offer excerpts from current bestsellers as well as news, contests, and author interviews. Hot on their heels have come the on-line booksellers, from the behemoths Amazon.com and Barnes & Noble to the corner bookshop, who have made buying books from all over the world a snap. If any further evidence is needed that the Internet is a reader's natural habitat, consider the fact that such on-line bookstores are currently among the few Internet businesses actually turning a profit.

In retrospect, the first edition of *The Book Lover's Guide to the Internet* can now be seen to have been a guide to just the beginnings of what the Net has become, and is still becoming, today. Many of those tentative first steps have grown into mature institutions on the Web. Others have, sadly, disappeared. (Many more have simply changed their addresses without leaving a forwarding address, and I've spent considerable time tracking them down for you.) A few of my favorite old hangouts on the Net, such as the global information network known as Gopher, have fallen as victims to technological progress, replaced by the newer and snazzier Web.

The good news is that for every site that has disappeared or gone dark, a dozen new ones seem to have sprung up. In revising this book, I have spent many (many, many) hours checking the accuracy of addresses of resources listed in the first edition and looking for additional sites to list. This should, by rights, have been a tedious process, but it wasn't. The more I explored the range of reading-related resources available today on the Internet, the more impressed and excited I was by the sheer dedication and inventiveness exhibited by book lovers in the age of the computer. It is impossible to visit some of the sites devoted to literature listed in this book and not come away with a renewed sense of optimism about the future of the written word in our society.

If I were pressed to name the most significant change wrought by the Internet over the last few years, I would nominate its enormously democratic effect, especially in rendering Net users' geographical location largely irrelevant. One of the best examples of this change that I can think of involves, not surprisingly, books. As a lifelong urban dweller, I have often wondered what it would be like to live in the remote country, many miles from any library or bookstore, with a limited (and quite possibly non-literary) circle of local acquaintances for company. Today, thanks to the community of book lovers on the Internet, the boundaries of intellectual and cultural life—its journals, discussions, bookstores, and correspondence—have expanded to encompass even the most remote points of the globe. I now know that, given an e-mail program, a Web browser, and a phone line, I could be happy in Outer Forgetaboutit. I'd just have to train the chipmunks to make bagels, that's all. But I'll bet there's a Web page somewhere that'll show me how.

Chapter 1

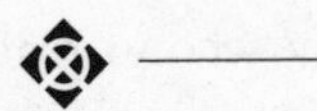

What Is the Internet, Where Did It Come From, Where is It Going, and Do I Get to Keep My Books When We Get There?

This is a book about books, reading, and the Internet: how to find books, magazines, newspapers, bookstores, and libraries on the Internet; how to find resources on the Internet of special interest to readers and writers; how to communicate with other readers and book lovers using the Internet; and how to use the Internet to publish your own writing.

The idea of doing this book came to me, appropriately enough, in a bookstore. I had already been exploring the Net for a while and had been amazed by the breadth and depth of reading material available on-line. So I was looking, that evening, for some sort of directory to fill in the gaps in my on-line explorations—a book about books on the Internet. Scanning the bookstore shelves for such a book, I realized two things. First, it occurred to me that the Internet itself was like a large but poorly organized bookstore or library, with thousands of volumes to read but no "Information Desk" and very few labels on the shelves. My second realization (after a prolonged but fruitless search) was that the book I was looking for, that Information Desk for the great on-line library that is the Internet, did not yet exist. Then a little voice said, "So write it yourself," and so I did.

Whether you're a newcomer to computers and the Internet or you're already on-line, this book is intended to serve as a sort of treasure map of the on-line world, charting a path to the remarkable literary riches to be found on the Internet. But before embarking on a treasure hunt, it's traditional to tell the story of how the treasure wound up where it is, and so we shall. Once upon a time, there was a little global computer network. . . .

WHAT IS THE INTERNET, ANYWAY?

Today almost everyone has heard of the Internet. Indeed, it sometimes seems impossible to pick up a newspaper or watch the news without being bombarded by nearly constant references to "the Net" or "the Information Superhighway." Even confining one's reading to the entertainment section of the daily paper is no escape—nearly every movie and restaurant advertisement is festooned with e-mail addresses and the cryptic "http://" hieroglyphics that signify a site on the World Wide Web. Nearly every magazine and television news show now encourages its readers to voice their opinions via Internet e-mail, and even the New York City Ballet has established its own toehold on the Web (**http://www.nycballet.com/**). (See Chapter 7 for a complete explanation of addresses on the Internet.)

What makes this sudden onslaught of Net madness all the more remarkable is that the Internet seems to have appeared and captured the public imagination virtually overnight. As recently as 1990, only a relatively small number of people, mostly those working with computer networks or at universities and research institutions, had ever heard of the Internet. A now-famous *New Yorker* cartoon of 1993, showing two dogs at a computer terminal (one saying to the other, "On the Internet, no one knows you're a dog"), was probably one of the first mentions of the Internet in a popular venue, and it almost certainly went right over most readers' heads.

So what is this thing called the Internet that has swooped down out of the blue and gobbled up the public consciousness?

Defining precisely what the Internet is has never been easy, and it's getting harder all the time. Perhaps the most important thing to understand is that the Internet is not a "thing" at all—it's more of a phenomenon than a physical entity. The Internet itself is actually a network of networks, separate computer networks all over the world that are connected to each other to form a sort of super- or meta-network. Some of these constituent networks are small; after all, any two or more computers hooked together can be called a network. In contrast, some of the networks connected to the Internet are huge—academic and corporate computer networks serving tens of thousands of users.

Because the Internet actually consists of thousands of smaller, sometimes private, networks, exact (or even approximate) statistics on the size of the Net are notoriously hard to come by. But as of early 1997, approximately 65 million people were connected in some fashion to the Internet, a number that is growing at the rate of 100,000 users per day. At this rate, there will be more than 300 million people on the Net by the year 2000. The Internet is *huge*, and getting bigger.

A Very Brief History of the Net

One of the curious things about the Internet is that it was never designed to be huge—quite the opposite, in fact. Ironically, today's wide-open and immensely popular Internet is a relic of the secretive and fearful atmosphere of the Cold War. The precursor of today's Internet was the Arpanet, created by the Advanced Research Projects Agency (ARPA) and funded by the U.S. Department of Defense in the late 1960s. Arpanet was designed to be a defense-oriented nationwide computer network capable, among other things, of withstanding a nuclear attack. The feared nuclear attack, thankfully, never came, and as the network grew over the years, it was gradually demilitarized, becoming a largely academic enterprise tying together researchers and students at colleges, corporations, and research institutions around the world.

Some of the features designed to permit the original Arpanet to survive nuclear Armageddon actually contributed to its gradual transformation into an extraordinarily versatile peacetime network. The durability of the original ARPA network was ensured by building in "redundancy"—data traveling from one computer to another could take any one of many routes to its destination. If part of the network were to be destroyed by a nuclear attack, the network itself would automatically route data by an alternate path. This clever little feature, carried over to today's Internet, makes effectively censoring the Net a daunting task: the Internet interprets censorship as a form of damage (who says computers are dumb?) and simply routes around it.

Arpanet was also designed to break the data stream transmitted over the network into little "packets" of information, like dividing a long letter into hundreds of individual postcards, so that if one packet failed to arrive at its destination it could easily and quickly be sent again. This method of sending data, called Transmission Control Protocol/Internet Protocol (TCP/IP), is the "language" spoken by every computer on the Internet today. This common language allows all sorts of computers—from PCs and Macintoshes to huge mainframes—to exchange data over the Internet. TCP/IP also makes it possible to transmit many streams of data over the same network simultaneously, a capability that comes in handy when there are millions of people on-line at the same time.

The Internet grew gradually over the 1970s and 1980s but remained largely an academically oriented, strictly noncommercial network until the early 1990s, when commercial Internet service providers made it possible for the general public to access the Net. The boom in home computer ownership in the late 1980s had already led to the enormous growth of "on-line services" such as CompuServe, Prodigy, and America Online, as well as thousands of local "computer bulletin boards," but these services remained completely separate from the Internet until about 1993. When the gates to the Internet finally opened to the general public, what had been a slow trickle of interest turned into a torrent of new Net users, then swelled into the tidal wave of public fascination with all things Internet we see today. And that, dear reader, is how your local car washing emporium ended up with an e-mail address and a Web page (if you think this is an exaggeration, pay a visit to The Car Wash at **http://www.defnet.com/car_wash/**).

But What Does All This Have to Do With Books and Reading?

Oddly enough, an aspect of the Internet that has been largely overlooked in all the media coverage is one that newcomers notice immediately: most of what you see on the Internet is text. The Internet is words, millions and millions of words. The unique riches of the Net, what a visitor can find on the Net and nowhere else, are, for the most part, things to read. The Internet brings together an enormous amount of textual information on nearly every topic under the sun, much of it either too arcane or too ephemeral to be easily found off-line. The Net can enhance your enjoyment of nearly any field of human endeavor—from cosmology to cosmetology, from rock music to foreign policy—but only if you're willing to read what the Net has to offer.

True, the cutting-edge technological wonders of the Net (pictures, movies, sound, etc.) may grab the attention of the mass media, but at their best they amount to little more than pale (and oddly pointless) imitations of television and magazines. Visit one of the Web sites maintained by the major movie studios, for instance, and you can download a ninety-second video file promoting the latest blockbuster—but why bother? If that same promotion appeared on television, chances are you'd change the channel. Visitors to one of the virtual art museums on-line (the Louvre is a popular destination) wait with high hopes for masterpieces to appear on their computer screens, only to be rewarded with fuzzy, colorless parodies of great art nowhere near the equal of the reproductions found in the most inexpensive magazine or paperback book. The same is true for the tinny sound effects and primitive video currently available on the Net—if that's what you want, television already does all that, and does it better. And although the interactive multimedia capabilities of the Net are bound to improve dramatically in the near future, the question for many of us will still be "Why bother?"

What makes the Net unique, what it does especially well, is the presentation of written material. There is a strong case to be made for the proposition that the people with the most to gain from the Internet today are readers—those of us whose leisure time is most often spent with a book, magazine, or newspaper, rather than in front of a television set or at the movies. For us, the Net offers what television, and even traditional books and magazines, cannot: a nearly limitless library of writings of every kind, most of which have never been published and all of which are now, miraculously, at our fingertips. For readers, the Internet is an enormous book, written by millions of writers all over the world.

The Internet itself, in fact, strongly resembles a book. The most popular part of the Internet, the World Wide Web, uses programs called "browsers" to present information to the viewer in the form of "pages" that look, lo and behold, just like the pages of a book or magazine.

BOOK LOVERS ON THE NET

For the book lover in particular, the Net offers a vast array of resources, many of which are only available on-line. The world of literature on the Net is much more than just "books on-line," although there are plenty of those. Project Gutenberg (**http://www.promo.net/pg/**), one of several "e-text" (electronic text) projects, has set itself the goal of putting 10,000 e-texts on-line by the year 2001. They may or may not meet their goal, but there are already hundreds of classics in the public domain (not covered by copyright) free for the asking on the Internet. Along with the well-known favorites of your school years, you'll find some of the more obscure works of famous authors on-line, making the Net's vast e-text archives a valuable resource for both the researcher and the casual browser.

Some of the resources awaiting readers on the Net mirror those available off-line, although the worldwide reach of the Internet can make it far easier to use them. It's possible, for instance, to order almost any book from dozens of on-line bookstores, whether you're looking for a current bestseller or a long-out-of-print rarity. Better still, thanks to the Web, you can now easily browse, and order books from, the catalogs of bookstores all over the world. Most major publishers also have Web pages, where you can search and order from their catalogs and often even read sample chapters of current bestsellers.

The evolution of on-line editions of general-interest magazines provides an especially interesting glimpse into the future of print publishing and the Net. After a tentative start on-line via The Electronic Newsstand (**http://www.enews.com/**), which allows visitors to sample an article or two from a variety of magazines, *The Atlantic Monthly* (**http://www.theatlantic.com/**) took the plunge and put most of the contents of each issue on the Web for free, even adding special "on-line-only" items for Net visitors. It is likely that many more magazines will make the jump to full Web editions in the near future, supported by revenue from advertisements on their virtual pages.

The Net also offers a wide range of genuinely new resources for readers to be found only on the Net—Web-based magazines and journals, on-line book discussion groups and mailing lists, Web pages devoted to literature and authors and discussions of their works, on-line literary and book reviews (many of which are listed in Chapter 7), and, behind it all, a remarkable community composed of book lovers and readers.

Many of the Web pages devoted to books and reading are treasure troves of information (and obviously Herculean labors of love on the part of their creators). A page devoted to the works of Mark Twain, for example (**http://web.syr.edu/~fjzwick/twainwww.html**), offers biographical and bibliographical information, links to electronic texts of Twain's works, information about mailing lists devoted to Twain, and links to other Twain resources (journals, archives, etc.). In the communal spirit of the Net, almost every such page also includes links to other pages on the Web devoted to the same or similar topics, plus often dozens of links to more general literary resources. Some of the most valuable pages for book lovers on the Web, in fact, are the indexes of resources, meticulously cataloging hundreds of links by author and genre. The page created by Piet Wesselman in the Netherlands (*Book Lovers: Fine Books and Literature* at **http://www.xs4all.nl/~pwessel**), for example, is a simply extraordinary collection of well-organized links to literary treasures around the world, and it rewards the visitor with hours of fascinating browsing.

Elsewhere on the Net, the emergence of serious Web-based magazines with built-in discussion areas, such as *Salon* (**http://www.salon1999.com**) and *The Utne Reader's Cafe Utne* (**http://www.utne.com/**), heralds the advent of Web content unavailable anywhere off-line. With these experiments, the Net has given readers something genuinely new: the ability to peruse a journal or newspaper on-line, then immediately participate in an informed discussion with other readers around the globe.

Literary journals and book reviews have also sprung up by the dozens on the Web over the last few years. Some of these are on-line versions of print publications, giving readers a chance to sample a variety of views not always available at the local newsstand. Others are entirely on-line; some produced by university English departments, many the work of small groups of dedicated individuals.

Similarly, the ability that the Web grants nearly everyone to publish his or her own writing in a highly visible venue has already produced highly creative personal Web sites showcasing poetry or prose, as well as intriguing experiments in collaborative fiction.

The dozens of literary discussion groups, e-mail mailing lists, and newsletters on the Net have brought the kind of in-depth discussions previously found only in literary salons or university seminars to a worldwide audience. Some of the Usenet discussion groups devoted to books and reading are probably visited on a regular basis by 50,000 or more people, and many of these groups have developed into on-line communities in their own right. It's not unusual for a single discussion topic in **rec.arts.books**, for example, to garner thirty-five to forty contributions from interested readers in a single week, and discussions of a controversial topic can sometimes last for months. **Rec.arts.books** is also the place to find periodic postings of FAQ (Frequently Asked Questions) files on a wide variety of book-related topics, including genre lists (such as *The Arthurian Booklist*, for devotees of Camelot) and the encyclopedic lists of bookstores in cities around the world compiled by Evelyn Leeper, who also maintains the extensive FAQ for **rec.arts.books** itself. Of course, **rec.arts.books** is only one of many Usenet newsgroups devoted to books—there are many other groups devoted to specific genres, such as science fiction, and to particular authors, from Anne Rice to Shakespeare (see Chapter 7 for a complete list of such groups). Each group brings together newcomers and longtime fans, casual browsers as well as serious scholars, in an atmosphere of lively and informed discussion.

That the Internet has proven a fertile medium for readers and book lovers is not really surprising, given its history as a largely academic network intended to facilitate communication between researchers and scholars. Years before the first "newbie" (new Internet user) from America Online dipped his toe in the waters of the Net, the Internet was being used every day to exchange scientific information, to communicate between libraries, to discuss literary theory and cultural trends, and to share research data between institutions thousands of miles apart. Consequently, there was already an enormous reservoir of often highly sophisticated literary resources on-line before the Internet "went public." Behind the glitz and silliness of the "multimedia extravaganza" view of the Net touted by the mass media, this "old Internet" is still chugging along, growing every day.

THE CULTURE OF THE NET

Not only did the Internet exist long before it was discovered by the average citizen, but the inhabitants of the Net had developed over the years a distinct, genuinely intellectual culture embodying many of the best (and, yes, a few of the worst) traits of its academic origins.

First among the virtues of the culture of the Net is a respect for the free dissemination of information and knowledge. Almost all Net users are passionate defenders of the principle of freedom of speech—so passionate that most of the great debates that have taken place on the Net have centered on attempts to muzzle speech on-line, either by other Net users or by governments. Even offenders against the peace and sanity of the Net as a whole—such as the obnoxious "net kooks" who blanket the discussion groups of the Net with their rantings on a variety of imaginary grievances—are granted, by and large, the right to do so.

The Internet community is also a fairly remarkable experiment in democracy in action. Because the Internet is arranged as a network of networks intersecting at a variety of points, there really is no "center" to the Net, and certainly no "Internet Central" running the show. The government gradually gave up its central role in the development of the Net in the late 1970s, and even the National Science Foundation, which had funded the development of the primary network "backbone" of the Internet, has now bowed out of the picture. The Internet today is a largely self-governing community. In place of regulations legally governing what can and cannot be done on the Net, there is "netiquette," a framework of unwritten common law generally agreed upon by Net users that keeps things running fairly smoothly.

A Few Principles of Netiquette

The basic principles of netiquette are simply Internet-specific elaborations of the Golden Rule:

• Don't do anything to other Net users that you wouldn't like done to you.

• Don't publicly post e-mail another person has sent you unless the sender gives his or her permission.

• Don't send your messages to inappropriate discussion groups—especially if you're selling something and you post your pitch to all 14,000 groups on the Net (a practice known as "spamming"). Never type your messages IN ALL CAPS LIKE THIS—doing so is the Net equivalent of shouting, and it is enormously annoying to your readers.

• Don't engage in "flaming" or "flame wars" (exchanges of hate-filled e-mail or discussion group messages).

• Don't waste Net resources: for example, don't copy a file from a computer in Japan when the same file can be found closer to home, or don't simply quote what someone else has said in a discussion group and then just add "I agree" to the end of your message.

• In short, don't do anything that your fellow Net users might regard as annoying or destructive. The Internet, for all its global reach, is remarkably like a small town in many respects, and those millions of people out there are your neighbors. Be a good neighbor.

What's Mine Is Ours

Perhaps the most unusual facet of Internet culture, and the characteristic in which it departs most markedly from off-line culture, is the spirit of communalism that prevails on the Net. The governing ethic of the Net has always been that the resources of the Net should be free whenever possible and that one should not take from the Net without giving something in return. The Net itself was built largely by volunteers, and historically many people have viewed the Net (and some still do) as a grand experiment in Utopian Communalism. Without delving into the ultimate practicality of that vision, it is still possible to be struck by the amazing amount of hard work that has been freely given to the Internet community by its citizens. It's not just a question of "free stuff" on the Net (although there's plenty of that). Many of the best sites on the Net, especially those having to do with books and reading, show an extraordinary love of knowledge, an eagerness to share it, and a willingness to spend months and years contributing to the commonwealth of the Net.

Growing Pains

The Internet, of course, is just a mirror of society as a whole and becoming more so every day. Unfortunately, some of the less attractive aspects of the Net have worsened of late, fueled at least in part by the opening of the Net to anyone who can afford or otherwise obtain a computer and a modem. What is called the "signal-to-noise ratio" (the proportion of content versus nonsense) sometimes seems to be dropping precipitously on the Net. The dominance in some areas of the Internet of a flamboyantly antisocial mentality, as well as a sudden influx of Net users who evidently view the Internet as just the latest incarnation of CB radio, has reduced some Net discussion groups to brutal and pointless shouting matches. The same yahoo factor has rendered Internet Relay Chat (the real-time chat facility on the Net) nearly unusable. And although pornography is not nearly as widespread on the Net as the mass media would have you believe, you'd never know it to judge by the number of "newbies" clogging some Net discussion groups with their requests for, as they put it, "nude pictures."

The World Wide Web, which has contributed enormously to the popularity and development of the Net itself, has highlighted another development on the Net in general and the Web in particular, which might best be called "the crisis of content." The sad fact is that much of what has been put up on the Web in the past two or three years is not worth the time it takes to access. The enormously democratic technology of the Web permits nearly anyone, anywhere, to put his or her thoughts and creations on the Net for the whole world to see. But this wonderful potential has led, sadly, to a global tidal wave of hundreds of thousands of pointless, sophomoric, and downright boring "personal home pages." The prevalence on the Web of such cultural detritus has become intense enough to earn the Web an unflattering but sadly justifiable comparison to public-access TV ("Wayne's Web," or simply "the World Wide Waste of Time").

Adding to the troubles of the Net in the last few years has been an extraordinary onslaught by commercial interests determined to "make a fortune on-line." Vast legions of hucksters who, in simpler times, would have been content to sell worthless oil leases or dowsing rods, have joined in a frantic Internet gold rush of such proportions that the arteries of the Net are becoming clogged with their ads. Network administrators have estimated that fully one-half of all daily traffic in Internet discussion groups, as well as a similar percentage of all e-mail traveling over the Internet, is now composed of commercial messages "broadcast" in the millions by "spammers" hawking get-rich-quick kits or pyramid schemes.

Whether the Net will survive this onslaught of mindless noise remains to be seen. One can only hope that it will, but, in the meantime, the trick to using the Net without having the urge to shoot your computer is to avoid the bad parts and seek out the good.

The good news is that there are true jewels amid the rubbish on the Internet, and there are more of them every day. The thousands of book lovers who engage in serious and civil discussions in Usenet groups are a very healthy sign. So, too, are the emerging cultural resources on the Net devoted to women's issues and the concerns of racial and national minorities. More generally, the increasing use of the Net and the Web to publicize campaigns on behalf of human rights and to oppose censorship around the world bodes well for the development of a global network of mature, responsible citizens, and the growing number of wonderful Internet sites created for (and often by) children augur favorably for the future of the Net.

There will always be a certain percentage of loudmouthed yahoos and hucksters on the Internet. But the history of the Net has also proven that there is plenty of room for the rest of us to construct a literate, humane alternative community on-line.

BOOKS, THE NET, AND THE FUTURE OF READING

Given the perilous state of literacy in our culture, the prospect of the Internet's becoming yet another vast wasteland competing with television for the attention of a nation of couch potatoes has deeply alarmed some commentators and educators. How can good old-fashioned books, they ask, compete with snazzy computer graphics? After we've all roamed the on-line world from our living rooms, who will be satisfied with a trip to the local library? Isn't the Internet really the final nail in the coffin of the written word? In many instances, these fears have been fed by the breathless predictions of chirping cyber-evangelists who seem to think that a bookless future would be a good thing.

One can hardly blame the critics of the Internet for being alarmed by the portrait of the future cheerfully painted by some cyberprophets, where libraries are supplanted by computer banks and the printed word exists only as an ephemeral image on a computer screen; where books themselves have been replaced by handheld computerized readers, and where even the need to frequent bookstores is obviated by the instantaneous delivery of "texts" over the omnipresent network; where electronic mail has superseded all other written communication, so that never again will we be burdened with trying to decipher a loved one's idiosyncratic handwriting; where true human memory has been replaced by data storage, and the cultural life of a nation can be loaded onto one giant hard drive; where society itself has fragmented into isolated individuals, numbly clicking their way from one "cool thing" to the next, bathed in the pale glow of a computer screen. One need not be a Luddite to find such a future appalling—as Samuel Goldwyn once said, "Include me out."

No one can promise that such a dire future will not come to pass, and it is true that there are, even today, some disturbing signs of the damage reliance on computers and "Internet mania" can wreak on the world of books and reading. Among them is the destruction of "old-fashioned" card catalogs at many libraries in favor of dubious data systems that often make it more difficult to locate a particular title. Alarming, too, is the fashionable but utterly fraudulent practice of rating the educational competence of a school by the number of computers found in its classrooms.

On the bright side, the dreadful vision of a truly bookless world is not likely to come true, at least in part because the technological wonders of the future are never quite as shiny and efficient (thank heavens) when they actually arrive as they were promised to be. Electronic books and the Internet are unlikely to ever replace real books, simply because real books are, and will continue to be, *better*. Books don't need batteries; books don't wear out; you can take books to the beach or into the bathtub (try that with a computer), and you can write an inscription in a book you love and then give it as a gift that has few equals in emotional significance. Human beings may not have meant to create something as wonderful and magical as books, and we certainly never dreamed at the time that we were inventing an "information storage and retrieval system" as versatile and adaptable as books, but we did, and it was a glorious accident.

We love our books and we're not about to give them up. The same goes for handwritten letters, and libraries with real books on the shelves, and bookstores where you can browse the shelves for a whole long afternoon. We have to be willing to fight to preserve these things because we know that they are, and will continue to be, important to human society.

The choice, ultimately, will be ours, because society is built by human beings, which brings us back to the Internet. The Internet is a computer network, largely accidental in origin, built in fits and starts from spare parts, and that's all it is.

The Internet is not now, and never will be, a substitute for, or even "a quantum leap" in, reading and education. Anyone who tries to tell you differently is selling snake oil, and trying to pick the pockets of future generations to boot. No one, least of all children in school, "needs" the Internet, any more than they "need" computers in the first place.

The Internet is simply a communication tool by which we can expand the experience of reading and learning by bringing resources and people closer together. The enduring contribution of the Net to reading and literacy is likely to be the discussion groups, research resources, and on-line communities of readers and book lovers that will add to our appreciation of, not substitute for, real books and the knowledge gained from reading them.

Chapter 2

Hooking Up: Simple Ways to Connect Yourself to the Internet

The first order of business for anyone interested in what the Net has to offer, of course, is to get connected to the Internet. Until just a few years ago, hooking up to the Net was a daunting proposition. Commercial access to the Net for individuals was virtually nonexistent, and even if you happened to have access through a university or similar facility, actually using the Internet usually required mastering the arcane syntax of the Unix operating system that serves as both the bedrock and lingua franca of the Net. Unix as a computer operating system has many advantages, but user friendliness is emphatically not among them, and clearing the Unix hurdle to get on the Net in the olden days (way back in 1990) often required making the acquaintance of someone known as a "Unix wizard" or "Unix guru." Wizards and gurus are not the hallmarks of a simple technology—after all, when's the last time you needed to go looking for a toaster guru?

But even in a world of increasing complexity, some things mysteriously get simpler, so brace yourself for some good news: Over the last few years, hooking up to the Net has become a genuine no-brainer. It is now much less difficult than programming a VCR, and only slightly more challenging than using a microwave oven. In fact, if you've bought a computer recently, and it came with a built-in modem, "jacking into the Net" may be as easy as plugging your computer into the nearest telephone jack. But even if your computer is an ancient hand-me-down from your daughter the chemical engineer, the Net is well within your reach. Best of all, you need never learn a single Unix command.

How you'll be able to hook up to the Net depends on who you are, where you live, and what sort of computer you own. In most cases, you'll have a choice of access methods among which you can choose based on how much time you want to spend on-line (and how much money you want to spend doing it). One of the best features of the Net, however, is the inherently democratic nature of the basic technology itself. We're all on the same Internet: the lucky fellow in a trendy Soho loft who cruises the Net using a $14,000 Silicon Graphics workstation hooked to a high-speed direct network link sees essentially the same *information* as the retired schoolteacher who uses an ancient 286 PC to dial into a freenet in rural Idaho. To squeeze the overworked Information Superhighway metaphor just a little, we'd all like to travel in a

Rolls-Royce, but there isn't anyplace you can go in a Rolls that you can't get to just as well in a Ford, or even a Yugo. If you're operating on a tight budget, you might not see all the bright colors and fancy graphics that the Net-privileged do, but e-mail, discussion groups, and mailing lists will look exactly the same to you as they do to Bill Gates himself.

EQUIPMENT

You really need only four things to access the Internet: a computer of some sort, a communications software program, a modem (a contraction of "modulator/demodulator," a little electronic device that allows your computer to communicate with others of its ilk over a telephone line), and a telephone connection. Each of these four basic requirements can be satisfied in a range of ways, from the simple (and inexpensive) to the arcane (and ruinously expensive).

If the prospect of buying a computer seems like too big a step to take right off the bat, you're in luck. It is actually possible to access the Internet (after a fashion) without a computer, software, or a modem, using a device such as a WebTV converter that hooks up to your television set. See "Internet Access Without a Computer" below.

Computers

Almost any sort of computer can be used to hook into the Net. I say "almost" only because there are some computers so thoroughly obsolete (the Radio Shack TRS-80 springs to mind) that trying to find communications software to use on them wouldn't be practical. Any IBM-compatible, Apple Macintosh, or Amiga computer, however, is a definite candidate for Net use. The only limitations of older computers are that the software will have to be text-based (rather than a graphic interface such as Microsoft Windows) and that the access (modem) speed supported by your computer may be somewhat on the slow side. You won't see any pretty pictures if you're using a text-only communications program, but there's a silver lining to text interfaces: they're much faster than graphic programs—fast enough that, in many cases, a text-only computer operating on a "slow" modem link will often actually deliver information from the Net much more rapidly than a fancy Windows program via a high-speed modem. Many folks who have access to graphic applications actually choose to use text-only programs for precisely this reason.

On the other hand, if you're considering buying a new computer, there are a few general points to keep in mind that will make your on-line life easier:

• Get as much memory (RAM) as you can afford. Many entry-level computers come with 8 megabytes of RAM, the minimum needed to run most World Wide Web browsers smoothly, but 16 megs of RAM will make your on-line life a lot easier, and 32 or even 64 megs would be a very wise investment. There is no such thing as having too much RAM, and having enough RAM is much more important than having the fastest processor on your block, no matter what the computer salesman tells you.

• If you buy a computer with an internal modem, be sure to get one that is at least 28,800 or 33,600 baud (baud is the measure of modem speed, roughly equivalent to bits per second, or bps). Make sure that the modem actually transmits and receives data at that speed: some computers are sold with fax modems that send faxes at 14,400 or 28,800 baud, but that drop down to 9,600 baud for data (on-line) connections.

• Get the biggest hard drive and the largest monitor screen that you can afford. A 17-inch monitor and at least a 2-gigabyte hard drive will repay your investment with freedom from eyestrain and anxiety. Peering at a small, dim screen while you worry about whether you have enough disk space to download that picture of the National Book Award Limbo-Dancing Finalists is no fun at all.

• Finally, some free consumer advice: Do not buy your computer at a store that also sells washing machines, aluminum siding, tube socks, or carpet remnants. Do not buy your computer at a store that sells only one brand of computer, or sells only brands that you've never heard of. And if the salesperson tells you that the monitor and keyboard cost extra, you're in the wrong store.

Buy a few computer magazines (*PC Magazine*, *Macworld*, and *MacUser* offer comprehensive comparisons of systems, for instance), browse through the ads, then either go to a reputable computer store or order your computer by mail from a major manufacturer. You'll be glad you did.

Software

To access the Net or on-line services, you'll need some sort of communications software, the program that controls your modem and presents the on-line world to you on your computer screen. There are a vast array of communications programs out there, and which one you use is governed largely by how you access the Net. If you buy a new computer, chances are good that it will come with the software for at least one on-line service already installed. If not, nearly every computer magazine these days comes in a plastic bag with a disk containing software from one of the on-line services. If all else fails, just call the service you're interested in and a representative will be thrilled to send you free software.

On the other hand, if you access the Net through an account at work or at a university, you either will be given or can easily obtain the requisite software from your system administrator. Community freenets (see page 32) usually leave it to their members to obtain their own software, but the folks who run your local system will be happy to point you in the right direction, usually toward a standard commercial communications program costing less than $100.

Independent local Internet service providers, another route to the Net, almost always supply free software with new accounts, although the "free" software is often "shareware," meaning that if you decide you like it and plan to keep using it (past about thirty days), you're bound by the shareware honor code to pay the developer a small fee (usually about $25).

Modems

As I mentioned earlier, a modem is the little gizmo that allows your computer to communicate with other computers over a phone line. If your computer didn't come with a built-in modem, you'll have to buy an external model that attaches via a cable to the communications port on the back of the computer. The phone line then plugs into the modem. Piece of cake.

Because the modem will be your link to the Internet, it's important to get the fastest model your computer can support. With a fast modem, images and text will snap up onto your screen, while a slow modem will give you plenty of time to make a pot of coffee while you wait. Even if you drink a lot of coffee, keep in mind that you may be paying by the minute for the time you spend waiting, so buying a fast modem can save you money. (This is a good argument to use on a Net-ignorant mate who'd rather use the money for something silly, like shoes for the kiddies.) Even if you don't end up paying by the minute, a fast modem will make the time you spend on-line both shorter and much more enjoyable.

Modems, like computers, have undergone a rapid evolution. In 1992, a 2,400-baud modem was considered reasonably zippy, but today 28,800 or 33,600 baud is the slowest modem you should even consider using. Fortunately, prices of fast modems have fallen substantially over the last few years, and a 28,800-baud modem (called a "twenty-eight-eight" by the Net cognoscenti) that ran $400 in 1993 can be had for less than $200 today. Resist the temptation to make do with a slower modem: the difference between a 14,400-baud modem and one running at 28,800 is more noticeable than you might think. The speed difference between a 28,800- and a 33,600-baud modem is, on the other hand, inconsequential. But it would be a good idea to go for the 33,600 modem because it may later be upgradable to a higher speed, while the 28,800 will probably not be.

While attempting to stay ahead of the technological edge in modem speed is probably ultimately futile, you might want to consider shelling out a little more money for a modem that receives data at 56,000 baud. There are two caveats to be aware of when considering a "56K" modem, however: First, while these modems do indeed receive data at (or near) 56,000 baud, for technical reasons they can only transmit data at a maximum rate of 33,600 baud. This sounds bad, but it really doesn't make much difference since you'll be receiving much more data than you'll be sending. Second, however, it is very important to make sure that your internet service provider supports 56K connections before you buy the modem; not all ISPs do (although your 56K modem will work perfectly well at a lower connection speed of 28.8 K or 33.6 K).

If you own an older computer, it's important to check whether it can support one of the new fast modems. Because of the configuration of their communications ports, some older machines may be unable to support speeds of more than 9,600 or 14,400 baud, so check your user's manual. If this is the case with your computer, the best approach is to buy the fastest modem your machine will support (with the consolation being that you'll be getting a bargain price on a new, but slightly slow, modem). If you end up accessing the Net in a text-only mode, you won't really be able to tell the difference in modem speed anyway.

As is the case when buying a computer, buying a modem from a reputable dealer is worth the effort required, and sticking to recognized brands is especially important. U.S. Robotics, Hayes, Supra, and Motorola modems are all good bets.

Telephone Lines

Obviously, accessing the Internet pretty much presumes that you have a telephone line to work with. Unless you're hooking up to the Net from an office or a university dorm room, you'll probably be using a modem to dial into a host computer of some sort that will be your gateway to the Internet.

About the only choice you have in terms of a phone line in most locales is how many to have. Keep in mind that anyone who tries to reach you while you're on-line will get a busy signal, so if you find yourself spending a few hours each evening on-line, you may want to look into getting a second line put in. Don't let the phone company tell you that you need a special data line for a modem—you don't. If later on you have problems with the line you use with your computer (especially excessive line noise, which can seriously degrade throughput, or data transfer speed), tell the phone company service reps that you use the line for a fax machine. They seem to understand fax/phone problems better than computer/phone glitches.

The lowly computer–telephone line hookup will be undergoing a major transformation over the next few years, one that will make any modem you own obsolete (go ahead—groan now and get it over with). The advent of home service high-speed digital, or ISDN (Integrated Services Digital Network) lines will double or triple current data transfer speeds. ISDN service is already available from phone companies in many areas, although the price of such connections is still rather high for all but the most dedicated Nethead. Still, we know that ISDN (or something like it, such as high-speed satellite-based wireless data links, or cable modems that use your existing cable TV wiring for Internet data) is probably the future of home Internet connections.

Of course, if you eventually decide that you *really, really like the Net a whole lot* (more than buying food or paying the rent, for instance), you may choose to sign up for a super-duper blazingly high-speed T1 or T3 data connection directly into the Internet itself. At between $1,000 and $3,000 per month, not counting the requisite hardware, this is an option you may want to sleep on for a while (and then discuss with your spouse, who will almost certainly tell you to shut up and go back to sleep).

INTERNET ACCESS WITHOUT A COMPUTER

If you listen to the cyberprophets (not something I'd recommend, in general), sooner or later you'll hear the term *Digital Convergence.* Simply put, this is the theory that sooner or later all our entertainment and communication appliances (computer, TV, radio, home stereo, VCR, telephone, answering machine, toaster, etc.) will slowly coalesce into one big digital doohickey, a stunning technological advance which will present consumers with the unprecedented opportunity to have absolutely every gadget we own go on the fritz simultaneously. Just imagine the thrill of trying to get a dial tone on your VCR while your telephone is erasing your e-mail. It's such a dumb idea that we can be fairly certain it'll happen.

Such fun is still a ways in the future, but the urge to merge all these devices has already produced one invention that may actually come in handy if you'd like to get a taste of what the Net has to offer without shelling out two or three grand for a personal computer. Internet/TV terminals, of which WebTV (**http//:www.webtv.com/**) was the first and is still the most popular, give the curious but uncommitted newbie a fairly inexpensive ($200-$300) and simple way to sample the Net without leaving the old BarcaLounger. These gizmos, small boxes that plug into the back of a standard television and hook up to a standard telephone line, allow users to browse the Web and send and receive e-mail on their TV screens all by means of a special point-and-click remote control. Aside from the cost of the box itself, the only expense is a modest service charge for Internet access (about $20 per month). For another $75 or so, you can even get a wireless keyboard to make typing and Web navigation easier, and newer versions of these boxes even include a port to which you can connect a printer. The design of the terminals also make it very easy to switch back and forth between TV and the Net by just pushing a button.

These nifty boxes have their limitations, and are not a real substitute for a personal computer: for instance, certain features of some Web pages (especially certain audio and video material) may not work quite right. But they do get you on-line, the technology is rapidly improving, and the price can't be beat if you're not sure that the Net is worth a major investment. If you later decide to spring for a full-fledged computer and modem, you can always bequeath the Net/TV box to your kids, spouse, or parents. Or you could try hooking it up to your toaster.

GATEWAYS TO THE INTERNET: HOW TO PICK A SERVICE PROVIDER

Once you have all the equipment you need to connect to the on-line world, the next step is to find something to connect to—a service provider. There are many different types of service providers, offering different levels of access to the Net.

Free (or Nearly Free) Access to the Net

Picking a service provider to hook you up to the Net used to be fairly simple: if you worked for a university, a research lab, a government agency, or a defense contractor, you were automatically wired into the Net, because these institutions thought it important that their employees and students be able to communicate via the Net. Of course, the only people to talk to on the Net were other folks who worked for universities, government agencies, etc., but even at this early stage many folks decided that the Net was very cool. The practice of university graduate students prolonging their connection to their alma mater simply to feed their Net habit was (and still is) not uncommon.

Many users still access the Internet via an account at one of these institutions. (Exact statistics on Net usage are notoriously hard to come by, but institutional access is especially prevalent outside the United States, Canada, and Europe, as commercial on-line services are only gradually appearing in most of the world.) In many cases, users of these academic or corporate systems also can connect from home by dialing into their work computers and jumping from there to the Net.

All this is relevant for two reasons. First, you may already be a winner: if you work at an institution or corporation that uses a local-area network (LAN) to tie its workstations or PCs together, ask your system administrator if you can access the Net from your desktop computer. Believe it or not, some employers actually think that giving their employees Net access is a good idea (although there may well be restrictions placed on what parts of the Net employees are allowed to access from work).

Second, if you're a graduate of a nearby university, you may be eligible for a dial-up account on your alma mater's system, which is almost certainly a gateway to the Net. Some especially savvy universities have begun to offer Internet accounts to alumni who pony up contributions to the annual fund-raising drive. Just call the alumni office and ask if yours is among them (don't flinch—after all, you don't have to give your name unless they say yes).

If you do manage to swing this kind of account, it's

possible that it will be text only, but, if nothing else, it's a good way to test the waters of the Net.

If you don't happen to work for the Defense Department or the like, your boss won't let you explore the Net from your desk, and an account with a university is not an option, your next stop should be the local freenet, if your community is lucky enough to have one. Freenets, as the name implies, are free bare-bones Internet service providers, often subsidized by local governments and businesses. They're more common in the rural west and midwest, but the trend toward universal publicly available Net access is one whose time (we hope) has come. Your local library is probably the best place to ask about an available freenet—in fact, libraries in many cities and towns now have open-access Net terminals available for use on a walk-in basis at no charge.

Many cities and large towns also have local bulletin board systems (BBSs). BBSs are small systems (often run out of the owner's home) that cater to discussions among members on a variety of topics and usually offer software libraries and games. Many BBSs are inexpensive or free to join, and some have limited connections to the Internet (typically only e-mail). *Computer Shopper* magazine carries listings of the thousands of small BBS systems in the United States.

Commercial Internet Services

If you're not eligible for any of the free or very low cost options discussed above, you'll have to bite the bullet and pay for access to the Internet. Sobering as this prospect may seem (who needs another expense?) it's just a matter of perspective—after all, a premium account with unlimited hours on a first-class service provider will still probably cost you less per month than cable TV.

Obtaining commercial Internet access is usually just a matter of choosing between two principal alternatives: the large national (and in some cases international) on-line services and an increasingly broad range of Internet Service Providers, or ISPs.

ON-LINE SERVICES

On-line services, such as America Online, CompuServe, and the Microsoft Network (MSN) have become so visible in popular culture that an introduction seems unnecessary. America Online (also known as AOL) in particular seems to have decided to take all our minds off the problem of global warming by threatening to bury us beneath a worldwide ten-foot-deep layer of its ubiquitous free software disks.

Surveys have shown that thanks to the on-line services' advertising barrage of the last few years, the average consumer is now hopelessly confused about the relationship between the on-line services and the Internet. Most people assume that the big on-line services *are* the Internet. But the on-line services and the Net are, emphatically, not the same thing. Until quite recently, in fact, the on-line services had, quite literally, no connection to the Internet at all. Each on-line service was a kingdom unto itself, and even sending e-mail from one service to another was often difficult or impossible. With the growth of the Net, on-line services have gradually opened up to the outside world of the Internet, thus giving their customers access to the wide variety of resources available on the Net.

While the Internet itself is a global network of networks with no center, each of the on-line services has a definite center: the huge mainframe computers that form its foundation. Each of the on-line services is a distinct network to which you connect your home computer over a telephone line. Only subscribers can access the features found on the on-line services.

Each on-line service, though you'd never know it from their advertisements, offers pretty much the same standard features: news, weather, and sports reports; on-line versions of popular magazines and newspapers; an on-line encyclopedia; forums or discussion areas devoted to a wide variety of topics, hobbies, and interests; and, of course, extensive computer sections with listings of software available for downloading. Most services also feature "chat rooms," or real-time discussion areas where subscribers can converse (by typing) with anyone else who happens to be on-line at that time.

All the major on-line services now boast some form of gateway to the Internet, although not all of them give their customers access to all of the features of the Net. These services also supply some sort of World Wide Web browser program, e-mail, and some form of software to read Usenet newsgroups (Internet-wide discussion groups).

The pros and cons of subscribing to one or another of these services are the topic of endless debate and beyond the scope of this book, but several points in favor of using them are worth noting, especially if you're a newcomer to the on-line world:

• Each of these services has a great deal of native content, features that are not available on the Net as a whole. Each offers a particular selection of newspapers and magazines, and several devote substantial space to book discussion groups, writers' forums, etc. Your best bet is to check the publicity materials for each service or enroll in a trial account (see below), and if something one of them carries strikes you as incredibly neat ("Holy cow! Plumbing Frontiers On-line!"), go ahead and subscribe.

• These services have prospered by making getting online a painless, nonthreatening experience, even for the most technically inexperienced user. If it's comforting to know that technical help is just a phone call away any day of the week, you may want to go this route.

• Recognizing that the Internet can sometimes be a confusing place for newcomers, all of these services have devoted a great deal of effort to making the jump from the cozy security of their service into the Internet as easy as possible. Help files and tips on everything from how to behave on the Net to how to find a particular site are offered to every customer. Anyone who actually reads all the informational materials these services offer their users before they access the Net will know more about the Net than many people who have used the Internet for years.

• All of these services offer trial accounts for a limited period in which to check out what the service has to offer. Getting a free trial account usually involves giving the service credit card information so that billing can begin as soon as your free time is used up, but such trial accounts can be a good way to choose a service that you really enjoy.

There are, on the other hand, some disadvantages to subscribing to one of the major on-line services:

• Customers of an on-line service are sometimes locked into using that particular service's proprietary software, which is rarely equal to the best Internet access software available. Some of the software is so poorly designed as to constitute a real barrier for users trying to access the Net. Stung by criticisms of their software, both CompuServe and America Online have reconfigured their systems to allow customers to use superior third-party software, such as the Netscape World Wide Web browser. Both services, however, still require users to use their e-mail software, which is vastly inferior to e-mail programs (such as Eudora Lite and Pegasus Mail) available on the Internet for free. In the case of the Microsoft Network, users' choice of mail software is more open, but users are restricted to one particular computer operating system—Microsoft's Windows 95 (or Windows 98).

• Because access to the Internet is routed through centralized mainframe computers and overburdened networks, customers often discover that using an on-line service is an infuriatingly slow method of surfing the Net. For example, Web pages that load in Netscape on a 28,800-baud SLIP/PPP connection in less than thirty seconds can take several minutes to load in the Compu-

Serve browser on a supposedly equally fast connection. Such delays can become a major source of frustration and, consequently, color your entire Internet experience.

Having said all this, I must note that a major on-line service is probably a good way to check out the Net and decide whether to proceed to a more direct connection. If you decide that you really like browsing the offerings of one particular service and only occasionally venture out onto the Internet, fine. Millions of people are happy doing just that. However, if you decide after a few months that the lure of the wide-open Net is too strong to resist, an independent Internet access provider is probably in your future.

In terms of a specific recommendation among the various on-line services, I would cast my qualified vote for America Online. While AOL has received a great deal of bad press in the past few years for its often substandard customer service (including what for some customers has amounted to a permanent busy signal when attempting to access the service), AOL has its upside, too. AOL has a much richer mix of content features than either CompuServe or MSN, including a large roster of periodicals which cannot be found on the Internet or other on-line services. AOL is easy to set up, easy to use, and is slowly but surely cleaning up its customer-service act. For book lovers in particular, AOL offers a vast array of message boards and discussion areas for readers of nearly any genre or interest, from classics to science fiction. AOL has also done a good job of integrating non-AOL Web content into its internal features, allowing users to seamlessly enjoy the best of both worlds.

Because the major on-line services change their terms of service fairly frequently, it's best to contact each service for information on current rates. Software for each service may be obtained via the following toll-free numbers.

America Online: 800-827-6364
CompuServe: 800-848-8199
Microsoft Network: 800-386-5550

Note to Parents

There has been much discussion in the popular media, and several genuinely alarming news reports, about the availability of pornography on the Internet, as well as the threat posed to children on-line by pedophiles. While in many cases the extent of these problems has been exaggerated, the concern felt by parents for their children's safety while on-line is entirely justified. A few points on this subject:

- The availability of pornography on-line has been overstated. While it does exist, it takes a concerted effort to find it, and the trend on the Net has been to make pornography more difficult, not easier, to access. Ironically, this is due to the desire of commercial pornographers to make money. Most sites on the World Wide Web containing pornography, for instance, now charge an access fee via a credit card, effectively barring most children.

• Most of the truly obnoxious visual material on the Internet is posted as multipart binary files in certain Usenet newsgroups. (*Obnoxious* here includes more than just sexually explicit images. Murder scenes and autopsy photographs are commonly posted in some newsgroups.) Fortunately, from a parent's point of view, the steps involved in merging, decoding, and viewing these files on a home computer are fairly technically complex; thus it is impossible for anyone to "stumble across" the material contained in these files. Unfortunately, several of the larger on-line services have seen fit to include the capability to easily and automatically decode and view these files in their latest software, thus making the process quite literally child's play.

• While the extent of on-line "stalking" and entrapment of children has been exaggerated, such incidents have happened, and parents should monitor children's access to chat rooms. In general, questionable behavior by other users should be reported to the service immediately. Unfortunately, America Online, alone among the major on-line services, allows its users to create a functionally unlimited number of "screen names," or on-line pseudonyms, a policy that seems to have contributed to antisocial behavior on AOL. In fact, America Online has been singled out by child welfare advocates in congressional testimony as being a magnet for pedophiles, at least partially because of its policies on anonymity.

• Therefore, I must advise caution in subscribing to AOL if your household contains children or young adults. I would not, if I had a young child or adolescent in my home, allow him or her unrestricted access to AOL, and would subscribe only if I were sure that I would always be in a position to supervise the child's on-line conduct, including e-mail. On the other hand, the same caveat applies to the Internet in general—don't put your children on-line at all unless you're ready to sit right next to them as they explore the Net. America Online, to its credit, has instituted a Parental Controls feature that allows parents to restrict their children's access to parts of both AOL and the Net beyond. This is a very good feature—use it. But don't let it be a substitute for your own duty to supervise your children's time on-line.

If you're planning to connect to the Net through an independent Internet service provider (see below), there are programs now available at many software stores that can also bar access to certain parts of the Internet. Unfortunately, these programs cast such a wide net in barring anything that users might find objectionable that they often block worthwhile Web sites. So once again, the ultimate (and only) guarantee of your children's safety on-line is your awareness of what they are doing at all times.

There are many wonderful resources available on-line for children, put there by people who truly love and respect young people and recognize the power of the Net to educate and entertain (see *The Children's Literature Web Guide* [**http://www.ucalgary.ca/~dkbrown**] for example). The benefits of the Internet are definitely worth the extra time and care it may take to make each child's on-line experience both happy and safe.

Independent Internet Service Providers

The last few years have seen the emergence of an alternative to the major on-line services: independent Internet Service Providers, or ISPs. ISPs sell access to the Internet, period. Customers dial into an ISP via a modem, and the ISP connects them to the Net. Connecting to the Internet through an ISP has several advantages over connecting through an on-line service like America Online, MSN, or CompuServe:

- ISPs almost always provide faster, easier access to the Internet than do the on-line services. As a rule, ISPs carry a full Usenet "newsfeed," meaning that users can access any newsgroup they choose, even obscure ones. Other aspects of the Net, such as file transfers and IRC (don't panic—they're explained in Chapter 3), are often also easier and faster to access through ISPs.

- Most ISPs now offer inexpensive SLIP/PPP accounts. A SLIP (Serial-Line Internet Protocol) or PPP (Point-to-Point Protocol, a newer version of SLIP) connection hooks your computer directly into the Internet, making for a substantially faster link than is possible through an on-line service. In addition, a SLIP/PPP connection allows you to use state-of-the-art Internet software (such as the Netscape and Mosaic Web browsers), newsreaders (such as Forte's excellent Agent program), and e-mail programs (such as Qualcomm's Eudora). Best of all, with a SLIP/PPP connection you can pick and choose among hundreds of free or shareware programs available on the Net itself. The most dramatic advantage of a SLIP/PPP connection, however, is speed. The difference between waiting for a Web page to load via one of the on-line services' poky proprietary Web browsers and seeing the same page snap up on your screen in Netscape is breathtaking, and can make the Internet a far more inviting place to visit.

(Some versions of the on-line services' proprietary software now also run on SLIP/PPP connections, giving customers of those services the same advantages, in theory, as those enjoyed by users who connect to ISPs via SLIP/PPP. In practice, on-line services' customers are still connecting to the Internet via the services' often overloaded networks, making even a PPP connection to CompuServe, for instance, run appreciably slower than one to an independent ISP.)

There are a couple of factors to consider when deciding whether to use an ISP, especially for newcomers to the on-line world:

• You should be aware that in opting for an ISP you're giving up the buffer between you and the Net that an on-line service provides. When you connect to an ISP, there is no "there" there—no homey welcome screen, no helpful tips, no on-line customer service department hovering at your elbow, waiting to lead you on a guided tour of the Net. You're simply connected to the Internet in all its glorious anarchy. This can be a disconcerting experience for novices. On the other hand, keep in mind that any reputable ISP will have a help line that you can call with your questions, and if all else fails, the Internet itself is full of folks who love to help newcomers.

• Setting up a SLIP/PPP connection can be more complicated than installing the software for an on-line service. Typically, your new ISP will provide you with disks containing a TCP/IP dialer (pay no attention to all these acronyms—it's really not that complicated), plus rudimentary mail and news programs and a Web browser. Setting up the TCP/IP dialer can be (but usually isn't) a bit tricky. If you're brand-new to computers or modems, make sure that the ISP you choose is willing to walk you through the process of setting up—any reputable ISP will be glad to help.

Depending on where you live, you'll have your choice of anywhere from one to twenty local ISPs, plus several national providers. There are good providers and bad providers, and the trick is to separate the two. Word of mouth is probably your best clue: a bad provider gets the reputation it deserves rather quickly. If you already have access to the Internet (via an on-line service or a friend), the best places to find information and opinions about Internet service providers are the **alt.internet.services**, **alt.internet.access.wanted**, and **alt.online.services** Usenet newsgroups. If you have a question about a specific provider, just post it in one of these groups, and chances are good you'll get an earful, both pro and con.

If you have access to the World Wide Web, there's a very handy Web page called *The List* at **http://www.thelist.com/**, which includes nearly all the ISPs in the world, organized by country and area code. Entries for the providers include area codes served, services offered, prices, and telephone numbers. A few minutes spent browsing *The List* will probably produce at least one likely candidate.

If you have no Net access yet, your best bet in finding a local or regional ISP will probably be a quick search of newspaper ads and local bookstores—there are several directories of Internet service providers available.

Another possibility would be to contact a national service provider, such as Earthlink (818-296-2400) or Internet MCI (800-550-0927), which offers SLIP/PPP connections in most areas of the United States.

The good news is that, with so much competition in the field, prices for Net access are almost certain to fall in the near future. On the other hand, the volatility of the market means that no guide, not even this one, can keep pace with all the new options for Internet access. But with just a little investigation, chances are good that you'll find an even better deal than the ones I've outlined. You might even get a month's worth of free car washes in the bargain.

Specialty Providers for Readers and Book Lovers

As the Internet gradually merges into the mainstream of modern life, we can expect to see a dramatic increase in the number of ways to hook up to it. Already the large cable TV companies, telephone companies, and on-line services are wrestling over prime cuts of what promises to be the largest communications cash cow since the invention of television. And they all have big plans for the humble little Internet. Already, as we've seen, the average couch potato can, using a set-top device such as WebTV, surf the Net on his 64-inch television from the comfort of his BarcaLounger, brewski in one hand, combination remote control and mouse in the other. The convergence of television and the Net, we are told, is inevitable.

Aside from whether such a development is in any way "inevitable" (after all, back in the 1950s it was said to be "inevitable" that we would all own personal helicopters "in a few years"), it is evident that it won't be that simple. The Net has already become many different things to many different groups of people, and a small industry is beginning to emerge based on the market for specialized niche Net access. Some of these services have been around long enough to have built real virtual communities among users who share common interests. We can only hope that these "small towns" along the Information Superhighway will be spared by the bulldozers of Digital Convergence.

Some of the newer specialized on-line services are aimed at businesses, charge hefty fees for access, and are unlikely to be of interest to individuals living on a fixed budget. These services include sophisticated data search and retrieval services and, in a cheerfully Orwellian marketing ploy, "personal news delivery services" that deliver a customized digital daily "newspaper" composed only of "news" that matches their clients' individual interests. If you actually enjoy the element of surprise inherent in reading your daily newspaper, chances are that such a service is not for you.

At the other end of the spectrum of specialized providers are the broadly based networks, such as PeaceNet,

EcuNet, and others catering to a particular spiritual or political constituency. Fees for these services are roughly comparable to those of mainstream on-line services, and details of each service can be found by searching Yahoo! (**http://www.yahoo.com**) under either the name of the service, if known, or the general constituency (clergy, activists, etc.) it serves.

As yet, there is no national on-line service specifically tailored for book lovers and readers in general, but if your primary interest on the Internet is serious and informed conversation about books and culture (as well as access to everything on the Internet in general), there is one service that merits consideration—The WELL, based in Sausalito, California.

The WELL was started in 1985 as a local system in the San Francisco Bay Area by the same people who produced *The Whole Earth Catalog* in the late 1960s and 1970s (the name is actually an acronym for "Whole Earth 'Lectronic Link"). Over the years, The WELL has grown into a remarkable on-line community of artists, writers, journalists, poets, and independent thinkers of all trades. At the heart of The WELL are its more than 260 members-only "conferences," or discussion areas, on an amazing variety of topics, ranging from books, writing, media, and poetry to popular culture and UFOs. Discussions on The WELL are lively, well informed, and, in the case of some topics, go on for years. Many of the contributors to The WELL conferences on books and writing are themselves established writers, whose work appears in such magazines as *The New Yorker*, *The Atlantic Monthly*, and *Harper's*—and is often discussed and dissected on The WELL shortly thereafter. The tone of conversations on The WELL is educated and intelligent—a welcome change from what you'll find on the large on-line services and, too often, on the Net in general.

For many years, reaching The WELL from outside California required either a long-distance call or a separate Internet account from which one could telnet (log in remotely—see Chapter 3) into the system. Once there, WELL users were faced with a text-only interface that might best be described as idiosyncratic. Recently, however, The WELL established its own national network, offering access to itself and the rest of the Net via SLIP/PPP connections from most major U.S. cities. The WELL has also introduced a World Wide Web interface to its conferencing system, which, although slower than the text system, is much easier for newcomers to master and enjoy. Although the Web interface to The WELL conferences is open to WELL subscribers only, The WELL home page on the Web (**http://www.well.com**) offers descriptions of all the conferences and a good sense of what The WELL is like.

If you already have an Internet connection of some sort, you can access The WELL via either telnet or the Web for $15 per month for unlimited time on-line, an option that I would nominate as the best bargain on the Net. The WELL can be reached at 415-332-9200 or by e-mail at **info@well.com**.

There may be smaller regional conferencing systems or bulletin boards similar to The WELL in your area, so it's worth checking around and possibly asking at your local library. One such system in New York City, Echo, was founded in 1990 and now has approximately 3,000 users and a lively roster of about fifty conferences on various topics going on at any given time. Stacy Horn, the founder of Echo, has been a leading figure in the drive to popularize the on-line world among women, and Echo remains notable among on-line services for the high percentage of women among its users. Being located in Manhattan gives Echo both a particularly "New York" tone and the opportunity to make use of local talent—the *Ms.* and *Village Voice* conferences are both hosted by the staffs of those publications. Currently, access to Echo from outside the New York area is available only by a long-distance telephone call, unless you already have an Internet connection, in which case, once subscribed to Echo, you can telnet into the system (**telnet://echonyc.com**) from your local Internet account. For more information, Echo can be reached at 212-292-0900 or at **info@echonyc.com**.

Finding the connection to the Internet that best suits your needs and tastes is, ultimately, a process of trial and error. Many Net users who now connect through a SLIP/PPP or even an ISDN link first got their feet wet by subscribing to one of the large on-line services. I myself had accounts with three on-line services and two different Internet service providers before I settled on my current connection (a SLIP/PPP hookup through Interport, a very good ISP in New York City, through which I reach The WELL in California). It's worth shopping around for a good connection, but don't let the wide range of choices get you down—sooner or later you'll end up where you want to be, and you'll have learned a great deal along the way.

Chapter 3

Getting There from Here: The Many Paths Through the Internet

The Internet, like our familiar physical network of roads, carries all sorts of traffic. Most public attention in the last few years has focused on the flashy stretch limo of the infobahn, the World Wide Web with its glamorous graphics. But the Net also has its own lumbering trucks, economy cars, and even bicycles. And just as a charming mountain cabin may be accessible only via a lowly four-wheel-drive vehicle, many of the best spots on the Net can only be reached with some of the older and simpler technologies (stretch limos don't do well on dirt roads, after all). A familiarity with a variety of methods of finding and fetching information can take you off the beaten path to some remarkable things hidden deep in the forests of the Net.

Here, then, is a brief overview of the primary ways to peek into the nooks and crannies of the Net. In keeping with the nature of this book, I have chosen to make my explanations fairly brief and nontechnical, as there are many sources of more detailed information easily available. Two other methods of information retrieval, Usenet discussion groups and e-mail mailing lists, will be discussed a bit further on, in their own respective chapters.

THE WORLD WIDE WEB AND ITS SEARCH ENGINES

The World Wide Web is the technology primarily responsible for the explosive growth of the Net over the last few years and is probably what most people think of when the Net comes to mind. The Web is the dazzlingly graphic part of the Net—the part that looks like a page in a book or a magazine, usually complete with pictures and fancy layout. When your dentist sends you a postcard telling you that he now has a site on the Internet where you can read all about gum disease, it's a near certainty that he's set up a "home page" on the Web. What makes the current status of the Web as the 500-pound gorilla of the Internet all the more remarkable is that it literally did not exist before 1990, and didn't really get going until 1993. Invented by scientists at the European Particle Physics Laboratory in Switzerland (known as CERN), the Web is a *hypertext information system*, which calls for a little explaining.

Hypertext is a method of linking documents together by means of reference points (called "links," naturally) embedded in the text of each document. Imagine, for example, that I have written a scholarly paper on bats, and at a certain critical point in my article I announce that anyone who doubts my findings should read "page 13 of Professor Rufus T. Firefly's seminal work *Bats Are Me*, available at the National Bat Archives of Freedonia." If I have constructed my paper as a hypertext document and made it available on the Web (and presuming Professor Firefly has done the same), the reader need only click his or her mouse on the highlighted title of the Professor's opus to be instantly transported, not only to the renowned National Bat Archives in far-flung Freedonia, but to the very dissertation in Professor Firefly's extensive oeuvre that proves my point. Hypertext, in theory at least, makes footnotes obsolete.

The Web is essentially a collection (a very large collection, mind you) of such hypertext documents linked together. The technology used to navigate among these documents and to bring them to your home computer is known as Hypertext Transfer Protocol, or HTTP. The revolutionary nature of the Web lies in the power of HTTP to link every document on the Web to every other document without going through any one central directory or menu. Every document or resource on the Web can spawn multiple paths leading in nearly infinite directions directly to other documents—thus the aptness of the "Web" metaphor and name. The Web, like the Internet itself, has no center; any given document (called a "page," stored on a computer called a "server" at a "Web site"), with its links to other pages around the world, may claim to be the center of the Web with perfect justification. There is no "up" or "down" on the Web; there is only "round and round."

While the development of the Web was a revolution in the organization of information on the Internet, the Web itself didn't really take off in the popular imagination until some folks at the National Center for Supercomputing Applications (NCSA) invented a little program called Mosaic in early 1993. Until Mosaic came along, the Web looked pretty much like everything else on the Net—line after line of text. Mosaic was the first graphic Web browser, and that "graphic" made all the difference. A page on Mosaic, or later graphic browsers such as Netscape and Microsoft Internet Explorer, looks like a page in a book or magazine, complete with pictures, fancy type styles, and background colors and textures. Graphic Web browsers also made it much easier to navigate among the myriad interconnected pages of the Web. Hypertext links on a Web page viewed with a graphic browser appear as underlined words or phrases, and once a link is "visited," it will usually appear thereafter underlined in a different color—the high-tech equivalent of trailing a thread to avoid being lost in the labyrinth of the Web.

Mosaic was an immediate hit with Net users, and, more important, with the general public. Millions of home computer users who wouldn't have dared to try to navigate the spartan and confusing "old" Internet were instantly fascinated by Mosaic and the Web. With the advent of the Web and graphic Web browsers, the Internet was finally ready for prime time.

The technology of Web browsers is still evolving at an astoundingly fast pace. The makers of the Netscape browser, in particular, have been instrumental in popularizing a wide range of bells and whistles for Web browsers, such as image maps (pictures coded to take the viewer to various sites when clicked), secure transaction forms (allowing the purchase of goods and services over the Web), and a variety of formatting codes that allow designers to create visually striking Web pages. Consequently, Netscape has become the browser of choice on the Web, though Microsoft's Internet Explorer browser is rapidly catching up to Netscape in the hotly contested "browser battle" for market dominance.

The Web and its graphic browsers have also made it much easier to navigate the non-Web parts of the Internet. Many of the features of the Net that previously were relatively obscure or required mastery of the forbidding Unix interface have been given new legs by the development of goof-proof Web interfaces. It's now far easier to search for and subscribe to a mailing list on a given subject (*Publicly Accessible Mailing Lists*—**http://www.neosoft.com/internet/paml**), or scan all Usenet newsgroup postings for a certain word (*Deja News*—**http://www.dejanews.com**), or locate someone's e-mail address (several methods are available at the *All-in-One Search Page*—**http://www.albany.net/allinone/**) than it used to be, all because these tasks are now possible via simple Web interfaces.

To say that Mosaic, Netscape, and their successors have revolutionized the Web would be like saying that television revolutionized modern life. Graphic Web browsers have proven to be genuine "killer apps"—software applications that make the underlying technology, in this case the Net itself, a "must-have," much as word processing programs drove the original personal computer boom in the 1980s. Within the last three years, the number of Web pages on the Net has rocketed from a few hundred to several million. The relatively simple technology required to produce and present a Web page has enabled everyone from telecommunications conglomerates to elementary school students to put up a page, or two, or a dozen. And, in a sort of hypertext evangelism, nearly every page has at least a few links to other pages, multiplying the possible pathways through the Net several times over.

The lack of hierarchical organization that comes with this infinite number of hypertext links is both the blessing and the curse of the Web. The ability to link resources separated by geography on one page has made it possible to assemble marvelous collections of literature resources from distant universities, for example, or to tie all the major on-line writing workshops together on one handy page. But the decentralized nature of the Web also makes it remarkably difficult to find your way around sometimes—there is, by definition, no one "right" way to get to where you want to go. Hopping from one page to another to another in search of a specific bit of information can be reminiscent of driving aimlessly about an unfamiliar city, often leading to the depressing realization ("Didn't we pass that doughnut shop a half hour ago?") that you're clicking around in a great big circle.

Search Engines

Enter the search engines and indexes of the Web. The Web was quite young, only a few thousand sites big, when a number of people realized that finding information on the Web was like searching for a needle in a haystack . . . in a hurricane. Web pages came and went (frequently when the college students who created them graduated), entire sites went off-line or simply disappeared, and once the Web really took off, new pages were being added by the hundreds every day. Something had to be done to bring some order to the chaos. There are now a variety of search engines (automated computer programs that scan for a specific term or subject) available on the Web, and while the Web may never be completely organized and indexed (and, after all, it wouldn't be such fun if it were), these search engines can help you get where you want to go.

One of the first, and probably still the most popular, of the Web search engines was Yahoo! (**http://www.yahoo.com**), developed by two graduate students in California. To use the Yahoo! search engine, you just type in the term or subject you're interested in, click on a "Search" button, and sit back and wait for the results, which will be presented to you as a list of links. You can then click on any one of the links to go to the site Yahoo! found for you. If Yahoo! itself doesn't find what you're looking for, you can click on links to other search engines and Yahoo! will submit your question to them automatically.

The great thing about Yahoo! (aside from the fact that it's absolutely free, of course) is that once you're there, you may discover that a search isn't really necessary. The staff of Yahoo! spend all of their time maintaining an enormous subject index of the Web in very simple outline form, so what you're looking for may well already have been found and indexed.

Other useful search engines are listed in Chapter 7.

Most of these utilities have options you can use to fine-tune your search (usually there's an "Options" link to click). Narrowing your search with these options will make for a quicker and more productive process.

The Web and Book Lovers

The Web and its rapidly evolving browsers have contributed enormously to the growth of the Net by giving what had been a forbidding text-only network a bright, open, visually appealing look. For the first time, what consumers saw on their computer screens didn't look like something on a computer screen—it looked like a book, or a magazine, or a catalog. And if it *looked* like a book, or a magazine, or a catalog, there was no reason why it couldn't *be* a book, or a magazine, or a catalog. This revolutionary potential of the Web was not lost on print publishers and booksellers, and, not surprisingly, a virtual stampede of booksellers, publishers, magazines, newspapers, writing workshops, and book reviews have rushed onto the Web in the last few years. Today it is a rare publisher or bookstore that does not have at least a minimal presence on the Web, and even small newspapers are scrambling to produce on-line editions for their readers.

One of the most remarkable features of the Web, the ability to link scattered and distant resources to a common page, has proven to be especially popular among book lovers. Almost every page having anything to do with books and reading on the Web, whether created by an individual, a publisher, a bookstore, or a university, is linked to other reading-related resources. The smallest bookstore's home page often carries links to the great libraries of the world, on-line writing groups, and, of course, other lists of reading resources. A virtual visit to a small bookshop in Maine may, within just three or four clicks of your mouse, land you in the Vatican Library or Trinity College in Dublin. And while "location, location, and location" may be the keys to a bookstore's survival in a modern urban setting, physical location and even global geography are irrelevant on the Web, giving a new lease on life to many beleaguered smaller bookshops who now, thanks to their Web pages, have access to a world-wide market.

Even when a Web page focuses on just a single work of one author, hypertext can add several dimensions to the reader's understanding of a book. A hypertext presentation of Jane Austen's *Pride and Prejudice* on the Web (**http://uts.cc.utexas.edu/~churchh/pridprej.html**) presents Austen's work extensively cross-linked to capsule biographies of every character, genealogical charts explaining the somewhat baroque family relationships in the novel, historical, geographical, and chronological background information for both the story itself and Austen's own life, helpful essays explaining the social conventions of the era, and even illustrations of key moments in the story.

The Web has also led to the development of entirely new kinds of resources for readers that could not have existed before the invention of graphic browsers. Hypertext collaborative novels, diaries, and history projects (see *Once Upon a Time in the Eighties* at **http://www.engl.**

virginia.edu/~enwr1016/ for an example), where the reader is invited to contribute to an on-line work-in-progress, are an utterly new feature on the cultural landscape. And conferencing systems (similar to bulletin boards), such as those maintained by *Salon* (**http://www.salon1999.com**) and *Cafe Utne* (**http://www.utne.com**) are, for the first time, allowing readers to talk to each other directly. The result has been the transformation of static print publications into living, dynamic forums for discussion. The truly revolutionary nature of the Web for book lovers may turn out to be the ability it gives us to talk back to the things we read.

The Web Marches On

Human nature being what it is, various people with a variety of motives have been trying to "improve" the Web almost since the beginning with new technological inventions. Applications written in the Java and Active X programming languages now allow the advertisements that litter many commercial Web pages to dance and sing almost as engagingly as the ones on television. Two recent developments in Web organization and technology, one possibly good, the other most certainly bad, merit special mention.

On the "possibly good" side are "Web rings." In principle, the idea sounds like a great one: since there are so many Web sites out there devoted to the same topics (cats, UFOs, Elle McPherson, and transformational grammar), why not link all the sites about a given topic together? That way, after you're through looking at one site devoted to Seinfeld, you just click on a link and you're taken to the next site, round and round in a big "Seinfeld circle." That's just what Web rings do, and over the past year or so they've sprung up in the hundreds, devoted to an equal number of topics, at least some of which are related to literature in some fashion. (A comprehensive directory of all existing Web rings can be found at **http://www.webring.org/ringworld/**.) The benefit of a well-organized Web ring is that it acts as a specialized tour guide—leading you from one site to another, based on your interests. A Web ring can take a lot of the bewilderment out of navigating the Web. The bad news about the good idea of Web rings is that there is very little quality control over sites that join the rings, and there are some real turkey sites out there in otherwise good rings. Still, Web rings are a logical way to try to organize the Web—just don't take them too seriously, and don't think that if you've seen one ring you've really seen what the Web has to offer on a given subject.

On the "terrible idea" front, we have "push" technology. The idea of push technology came from commercial Web sites that support themselves by selling advertising space. Every time you visit the CNN site, for example, your visit is counted and allows CNN to charge more for its ad space. But what happens if you get up one morning and forget to hop over to CNN? They lose money, that's what. So the Big Guys of the Web decided that they shouldn't be waiting for you to come to them when they could come to you, and "push" their content (and their ads) right onto your computer screen. The major Web browser makers (Netscape and Microsoft) thought that this was such a dandy idea that they have built this "push" capability into their latest generation of browsers. Users can now "subscribe" to large commercial Web sites such as CNN or MSNBC, and thereafter receive daily (and sometimes hourly) "updates" of the site's content every time they log onto the Net.

The danger of "push" technology is not that we'll all be bored to death by the constant updates (so far, we're still allowed to turn this feature off in the new browsers), but that the small, quirky, wonderful sites on the Web will be suffocated by users' reliance on "push" from the big commercial sites. The Web only works if Web users are willing to go exploring and stumble across new things. "Push" technology discourages exploration, turning the Web into a very slow version of television by feeding slick commercial content to passive viewers. We can only hope that there's enough feisty fighting spirit left in Web users to sit up in their chairs, click their own mouse buttons, and push "push technology" right onto the Great Internet Flop Pile.

FTP

Sooner or later, you're going to want to download something from the Internet. "Downloading" is the process of copying a file from a remote computer to your own home computer so that you can read it, work with it, or, if the file is a program, install and run it. Perhaps you'd like the latest version of Netscape—after all, the company seems to release a new one just about every week.

Or perhaps you've always wanted a digitized version of *Moby Dick* (but you'd better wait until the weekend—downloading the whole book could easily take hours).

Every on-line service has its own file libraries and download mechanisms, but out on the wild and woolly Internet, almost all file transfers are handled by a method called FTP (file transfer protocol). FTP is a very powerful and flexible method of transporting and managing files on the Net—not only can you download files to your own computer, but you can also upload files from your home machine onto a remote computer. If you establish a personal home page on the Web (see Chapter 6), for example, you'll probably use an FTP program to put up and periodically update the page.

In most cases, you'll be using FTP either through an interface supplied by an on-line service or through an FTP program running on your home computer via a SLIP/PPP connection. Most SLIP/PPP accounts will include a basic FTP utility as part of the startup package, and more sophisticated FTP programs are available as shareware on the Net itself. Many Web browsers, such as Netscape, can also handle FTP transfers automatically.

The most common use of FTP programs is to copy files from a remote computer (known as an "FTP site") by means of a procedure known as "Anonymous FTP." In Anonymous FTP, you're actually logging into a remote computer (using the word *anonymous* as your login name and your e-mail address as your password) and copying files to your own system. If you're using FTP through an on-line service, you won't have to worry about a login and password: the on-line service's system will take care of that for you. If you're using an FTP program on your home computer, just check the "anonymous" box in the configuration dialog box and you'll be in business.

To transfer files from an FTP site to your home computer, you'll need to know both the name of the file you're looking for and the exact directory in which it resides on the host computer. Fortunately, most magazine articles or Internet sites that mention a program or file that you might want to FTP will also give you the information you'll need in a standard addressing format—**ftp://ftp.twinkies.com/pub/neatstuff.txt**—or something similar. In this example, you'd FTP to the "ftp.twinkies.com" site, switch to the "pub" directory (which is where files available to the public are stored on many computer systems), then look around for a file called "neatstuff.txt." Just tell your FTP program where you want that file stored on your home computer, hit the "file transfer" button, and the rest is usually automatic.

FTP is one of the core applications on the Internet, and it's definitely worth the few minutes it may take you to master it. Besides allowing you to take advantage of the vast software resources available on the Net, FTP can fetch some of the best written resources on the Net. Any sort of long text file, whether a dissertation, a technical report, or a novella, will probably be too long to be found on a Web site or in a newsgroup. In cases like these, a basic familiarity with FTP will not only allow you to zip in and grab the file, but after downloading it to your home computer, will give you plenty of time to read the file off-line.

Two caveats apply to using FTP, however. First, remember that whenever you're connected to a remote computer system you're a guest there and that, in all likelihood, the system was intended for use by people doing serious work. If possible, conduct FTP sessions after business hours (whatever they may be where the host computer system is located).

Second, while there is almost no chance of accidentally acquiring a computer virus by downloading software from a corporate site or from one of the major shareware libraries on the Net, it's still wise to use a good antivirus scanning program before you run any program. Text and graphics files, on the other hand, pose no threat of viruses—viruses can only be transmitted in a program file.

TELNET

Telnet is one of the oldest applications on the Net and still one of the most versatile. When you "telnet into" a site, you're actually logging onto that computer as a user—what you see on your home computer screen is exactly what a local user on that remote system would see. Most often, you'll be presented with a text-only menu when you telnet into a system. If you're accessing the system through an on-line service or other graphic interface, a separate window will open up, usually showing white text on a black background, and a blinking cursor. Don't be alarmed; you'll always see instructions about how to log onto, as well as how to exit from, the remote system.

Telnet may not be the most glamorous method of getting information on the Net, but it is one of the most powerful, and there are some very neat things on the Net reachable only via telnet. Many library catalogs, for instance, are accessible only by telnet—the library itself may have a very impressive Web page with stately graphics and basic information, but if you want to know if it has a particular book or journal, you'll end up using telnet to find out. Telnet is also useful when you subscribe to a faraway bulletin board or conferencing system that does not have free local phone numbers in your area. Rather than calling long-distance to my account on The WELL, a system in California, for example, I can telnet in from my local New York provider, thus paying only the cost of a local call.

The particulars of how to access and use telnet will vary according to how you access the Internet, but the telnet system itself is refreshingly simple, and, once you get the hang of it, you'll find it to be one of the quickest and handiest ways to hop around the Net.

IRC (Internet Relay Chat)

Most of the Internet is "time-shifted"—while people communicate in a variety of ways over the Net, the messages are rarely transmitted and received in real time (i.e., simultaneously), as on a telephone. You post a message to me in a Usenet discussion group (see Chapter 4) or send an e-mail. I read your message the next day and send a reply, which you then read later that day or next week. A Web page may exist on the Net for weeks or months before anyone sees it (if ever), and many of the files accessible by

FTP or telnet have been snoozing peacefully on their home systems for years. For a cutting-edge system of communication, the Internet actually carries on its business at a remarkably pastoral (some would say glacial) pace.

There is an analogue of the telephone on the Net, however, that lets you talk (albeit by typing on your keyboard) to anyone who happens to be on-line at the same time, anywhere in the world. Internet Relay Chat (IRC) is a global real-time system of hundreds of channels, each with its own topic, on which thousands of people can "chat" with each other twenty-four hours a day. For many years, IRC was restricted to only the most technically proficient Net users by virtue of a confusing interface and arcane operating commands. Recently, however, a new generation of user-friendly IRC software (such as Khaled Mardam-Bey's "freeware" mIRC for the Windows operating system) has opened the world of IRC to newcomers to the Net. Some Web pages now also boast "gateways" to IRC chat via small Java applications that transform your Web browser into a graphic IRC application. Two you might like to try are Talk City (**http://www.talkcity.com/**) and Pathfinder Chat (**http://www.pathfinder.com/**).

IRC is enormously popular, as are the "chat rooms" (similar to IRC) maintained by all of the large on-line services for their users. The on-line services have acknowledged that the services' chat rooms are by far the most popular feature that they offer, and it is not unusual to find more than 1,000 IRC channels open and operating on any given evening on the Net.

Unfortunately, IRC sounds like a much more exciting place than it actually is. The level of discourse found there (and even more so in the on-line services' chat rooms) is relentlessly inane, often pointlessly obscene, and, worst of all, mind-numbingly boring. One newspaper reporter, after exploring the America Online chat rooms for a while, remarked that Dante, had he lived in the 1990s, would not have given his vision of Hell "rings"—he'd have given it "chat rooms."

There are, of course, exceptions, even on IRC. Pick a channel called "Friendly," "Pub," or "Callahans," and you'll meet a group of very nice regulars discussing a variety of topics. The folks on the "Over 40" channel tend to be kinder and gentler than the rest of IRC's denizens. There's even a channel called "Writers," devoted to chat about writing, although, because of the fundamental incoherence of IRC, sustained conversations of substance are very rare.

It's all a matter of opinion, of course, and to each his or her own. Evidently some people find IRC and chat rooms fascinating enough to have made the on-line services very rich (and to have necessitated the formation of a Usenet newsgroup called **alt.irc.recovery** to help wean IRC addicts). If, however, you have ever wished for a few extra hours in the day so that you could catch up with your reading, you're unlikely to be tempted to spend any substantial amount of time on IRC.

Chapter 4

Usenet Discussion Groups and Web Forums: Adding Your Two Cents' Worth

Much of the Internet is essentially a passive, solitary medium. Popular phrases such as *surfing the Net* may conjure up visions of acrobatic hotdogging, but the truth is that the average Net surfer's physical exertions amount to no more than clicking a mouse or typing a few terse commands and watching the results pop up on the computer screen. In most cases, there is no one home at the other end of that network connection: the Web page or FTP site resides on a remote computer, running unattended, delivering the same content hour after hour with all the warmth and personality of a soft drink machine. Much as Netters might like to think otherwise, sitting in front of a computer, clicking a mouse button, bears a disquieting resemblance to sitting in front of a television set, clicking a remote control. (Alone, yet. While communal television viewing provides an opportunity for at least some, albeit low-quality, socializing, very few families outside of computer ads actually gather 'round the ol' Pentium on a winter's evening.) The worst-case scenario of the explosive growth of the Internet over the last few years, heard with increasing frequency from critics of the Net, is that the entire on-line revolution brouhaha will ultimately breed a nation of "Net potatoes," vast herds of passive browsers wedded to their computers, cut off from all contact and conversation with real people as they click their way from site to site, caught in a Web of solitude.

If this dystopian view of the Internet and the on-line world does not come to pass, it will be largely thanks to those parts of the Internet that allow users to join in discussions with their fellow Net-users. These discussion groups and Web forums, which allow individuals anywhere in the world to post their comments on the Net for anyone else anywhere in the world to read and respond to, together constitute the most exuberantly anarchic experiment in collective free speech in human history.

These discussion systems fall into two main categories: Usenet "newsgroups," and Web-based conferencing systems and bulletin boards. Although these two kinds of discussion groups run on entirely different types of computer technology, they both permit users to read what other users have written and to post their own unedited (and usually uncensored) opinions. Both Usenet and most Web conferencing systems are also "time-shifted": that is, discussions take place over days or weeks with users posting their comments whenever they choose, rather than having to be on-line at any particular time in order to be able to participate. In this regard, discussions on these systems are much more convenient for participants (and often much more coherent) than those to be found in the "real time chat rooms" of the on-line services and IRC (see Chapter 3).

USENET NEWSGROUPS

Freedom of the press may belong, as the cynics say, to those who own the presses, but the beauty (and the genuinely revolutionary nature) of Usenet is that it gives anyone with a computer and a network connection the equivalent of not just a printing press, but a built-in worldwide audience of millions of readers.

Thanks to Usenet, I can roust myself out of bed at 3 A.M., compose a masterful analysis of the socioeconomic significance of the recent public fascination with the works of Jane Austen, post it to the relevant newsgroup (**rec.arts.books**) in a matter of five seconds or so, and crawl back into bed with the satisfaction of knowing that before noon the next day somewhere between several thousand and several million people will have read (or at least glanced at) my masterpiece. Usenet gives anyone with an Internet connection an ability to broadcast his or her opinion to the world unmatched by even the largest newspaper and television networks.

And broadcast we will. While it's possible to just sit back and watch Usenet scroll by, sooner or later everyone feels the overwhelming need to contribute his or her two cents' worth to the thousands of ongoing discussions that make up Usenet. The art of conversation is alive and well on Usenet.

Begun in the infancy of the Internet in 1979 as a way for Unix computer programmers and a few academics to share information over the fledgling network, Usenet (known originally as "Netnews") today encompasses over 20,000 different "newsgroups," each of which acts as a bulletin board devoted to a particular topic. (Occasionally you may hear an old-timer proclaim that Usenet is "not part of the Internet." Technically speaking, this is true, in that some sites that are not connected to the Internet do receive Usenet material.)

Although Usenet is made up of "newsgroups," there is very little of what most of us would consider "news" in the conventional sense on Usenet. But there are plenty of personal opinions—and opinions, often strongly held, are the essence of Usenet. Consequently, there are newsgroups devoted to nearly every topic anyone might have an opinion on, from cats to opera to poetry to mysticism to baseball to car repair. Within a given newsgroup, messages are posted on a variety of topics (called "threads"), most of which, on a good day, have something to do with the overall theme of the newsgroup. Any user who reads a posting (also called an "article") on a particular topic and has something to say on the subject can then reply to the first posting, or to someone else's reply, and so on, ad infinitum. Any user can also start a brand-new thread and then sit back and watch over the next few days as fellow Netters agree, disagree, or simply ignore the topic entirely. Replies are likely to roll in from around the world, and often in astonishing numbers. While low-traffic newsgroups may receive only five or ten contributions per day, some of the more popular often see between 300 and 500 new postings every day of the week—quite a change from the early days of Netnews, when the design specifications for the system that was to become Usenet estimated that the traffic would be a total of two articles per day.

Perhaps the most remarkable characteristic of Usenet is that, by and large, no one is in charge. Any article posted to a newsgroup is rapidly transmitted from the author's host system to thousands of computers (called "news servers") all over the world, each of which stores the article and makes it available to the users of that local system. There is, therefore, no "Usenet Central" that can pull the plug on opinions it finds offensive—with rare exceptions, no one can erase an article from the worldwide Usenet system except the author of that particular article.

That Usenet lacks a "master control" does not mean that anarchy prevails, however. Usenet has developed a singular communal culture over the years, complete with its own traditions, standards, folklore, and lingo. Not surprisingly, the users of Usenet have also collectively developed principles of netiquette (see Chapter 1 for an explanation of netiquette) spelling out what constitutes unacceptable on-line behavior. Posting advertisements (known as "spam") in inappropriate newsgroups (there are newsgroups set aside for this purpose), excessive "flaming" (posting insulting or obscene messages), posting messages having nothing to do with the topic of the newsgroup (lobbing singles ads into the **rec.pets.cats** newsgroup, for instance), and a few other notable transgressions are all violations of netiquette. Netiquette is informal but almost universally observed, and the penalties for violations range from flaming the offender to, if the offender is being seriously and consistently disruptive, complaining to whoever provides the offender's Net access (on-line service, university system administrator, etc.). If any access provider receives more than a few complaints about a given user, that user's access is almost certain to be yanked. Such a drastic solution is a rare occurrence, largely because Usenet users across the political spectrum are, almost without exception, passionate defenders of free speech. It also helps the cause of tolerance that most good newsreading programs (see page 91) contain a feature called a "killfile," which enables a user to ignore posts from known "Net kooks."

If you want your debut in Usenet to be auspicious, you'll want to spend some time reading the postings in the newsgroup created just to help newcomers get their bearings, called, logically enough, **news.announce.newusers**. If you have questions about Usenet or any other part of the Internet, post them in **news.newusers.questions**, and you'll probably get answers from all over the Net.

THE ORGANIZATION OF USENET NEWSGROUPS

The prospect of browsing through over 20,000 Usenet newsgroups to find just the ones dealing with your favorite topics of discussion may seem a little daunting, but don't worry. Newsgroups are organized into a remarkably logical (again, considering that no one is "in charge") hierarchy. The hierarchy is composed of eight main groups, each of which has numerous subgroupings, reflected in the names of the individual newsgroups. Seven of the top-level groups are considered the original, "official" Usenet categories:

comp.	computer-related
humanities	academically oriented discussions of culture
misc.	miscellaneous and unclassifiable topics
news.	Usenet and the Internet
rec.	recreational (hobbies, art, music, etc.)
sci.	science-related
soc.	social issues
talk.	general discussion on a variety of topics

Each top-level domain is divided into a family tree of groups, whose lineage can be discerned by the logical arrangement of their names, reading from left to right as they become more specialized. For example:

rec.arts.music
rec.arts.music.classical
rec.arts.music.classical.recordings

This branching-tree approach lends a welcome order to what otherwise would be a chaotic assortment of groups.

In the eighth top-level grouping are the "alt." (or "alternative") newsgroups, the domain of the wild, the wacky, and the often just plain strange. The alt. groups comprise the "unofficial" Usenet groups, and they differ from the original seven top-level groupings in several ways. The most notable is that while there are standardized and fairly rigorous procedures involved in starting an "official" newsgroup (involving public petitioning and voting, all taking place on Usenet, of course), anyone can start an alt.

group. All that a prospective founder of an alt. group (say, Joe Smith) need do is convince enough system administrators to carry the new group (alt.fan.joe-smith, most likely) on their news servers. The upside of this open-door policy is that it has led to the creation of some of the liveliest groups on Usenet—**alt.folklore.urban** and **alt.usage.english**, for instance, to name two of my favorites. The downside of the ease with which alt. groups can be set up can be seen in groups such as **alt.tv.dinosaurs.barney.die.die.die**. (not to mention **alt.sex.bestiality.barney**) and the consequent refusal of many system administrators (especially at universities) to carry the alt.* hierarchy of groups. Many on-line services do not include the entire alt.* hierarchy in their basic newsgroup offerings, although most will let you read them if you already know the name of the group. Most of the independent Internet service providers, in contrast, carry a full newsfeed (i.e., all 20,000-plus Usenet groups, including the entire alt.* hierarchy) and allow their subscribers to make their own decisions on matters of taste and morality.

Depending on the range of newsgroups your particular provider carries, you will occasionally see groups beginning with odd letters, such as **ny.** and **az.** These are geographically or institutionally local newsgroups mostly of interest to the people who live in that particular area or attend a particular school. My Internet service provider in New York City, for instance, not only carries the "**nyc.**" groups but also, for some inexplicable reason, newsgroups in the "**oh.*** " hierarchy, pertaining to Ohio. On a more useful note, a really good provider will carry the ClariNet newsgroup hierarchy (**clari.***), a commercial service that posts actual news from the Associated Press and other sources, in the form of Usenet articles.

Most providers also maintain internal Usenet groups, usually in a hierarchy beginning with the service's name (**interport.questions**, **interport.announce**, etc.). These groups are only visible to users of that particular provider, are usually monitored by the service provider itself, and can be a valuable source of information if you have questions about either the service or the Internet in general.

The vast majority of Usenet groups aren't moderated: anyone can post anything without fear of censorship or reprisal (except the possibly negative reactions of other users of the group). A few newsgroups, by common agreement among their users, are moderated; any posting automatically goes first to a moderator, who decides whether it is relevant to the purpose of the group. If it is, the moderator then forwards it to the general newsfeed for distribution. Moderated newsgroups have a higher signal-to-noise ratio than unmoderated groups but often pay a penalty in dullness.

Usenet being the remarkably self-organized place that it is, there is an information desk for nearly every newsgroup—the Frequently Asked Questions file, or FAQ—where newbies can get the lowdown on the theme, history, quirks, and quibbles of the group and its regular contributors before plunging in. Reading the FAQ for a group before posting there is one of the most important ground rules of netiquette and the best way to avoid making a bad first impression on the locals. Most Usenet groups regularly post their FAQs in the group itself every month or so, but a wide variety of FAQs are also always available at **ftp://ftp.rtfm.mit.edu/pub/usenet**. The "rtfm," by the way, stands for an old hacker catchphrase: "Read the (friendly, freakin', whatever) manual." It's good advice. Reading the FAQ will prove invaluable in helping you to avoid being roasted and toasted by flames on your first foray into a newsgroup.

USENET NEWSREADERS

The program used to read messages on Usenet (and to write and post your own) is called a newsreader. There are a wide variety of newsreaders in use on the Net, ranging in quality and ease of use from the ridiculous to the sublime, but the type of newsreader you will end up using will largely be determined by how you access the Net. All newsreaders allow you to "subscribe" to certain groups that you plan to read regularly; the other 19,985 (or whatever) groups are then hidden from sight, so you don't have to scroll through them every day to get to your favorites.

On-line services such as America Online and CompuServe include newsreading software in their all-in-one proprietary software suites, often hidden behind a button that calls Usenet by another name, such as "Internet Bulletin Boards" or "Discussion Groups." Most newsreaders of this type come preconfigured with a few start-up newsgroups, leaving it up to the user to pick additional groups to read. Some groups, especially those in the alt.* hierarchy, are often not listed in the service's master list of available groups, although they can usually be added if you already know the exact name of the group you want to read.

Unfortunately (and ironically, since these services stress

ease of use as a selling point), the newsreading software supplied by on-line services is almost always slow and awkward. It often also lacks basic features, such as quoting parts of the message you're replying to, forwarding a posting via e-mail, and sending the same message to more than one group (called "cross-posting"). If you're starting out on an on-line service and find Usenet a valuable and enjoyable resource, keep in mind that one of the advantages of eventually switching to an Internet service provider with a SLIP/PPP connection is the ability to use one of the vastly superior TCP/IP newsreaders on the market.

If you're accessing the Net through a university, free-net, Unix, or other text-based account, the newsreader you use will be dictated by the tastes of the person administering your system, since the newsreading software runs on the host computer, not your personal machine. The bad news is that whatever newsreader you are offered (probably a Unix program called TIN, RN, or TRN) will be strictly text-based and not very pretty to look at. The good news is that it will be much faster, more powerful, and (once you get the hang of it) easier to use than the newsreaders offered by the on-line services. Many experienced users with access to graphic newsreaders still prefer to use TIN or TRN.

If you're connecting to the Net through a direct network or SLIP/PPP dial-up connection, the world is your oyster, newsreader-wise. Depending on the type of computer you're using, there is a wide variety of TCP/IP newsreader software, both commercial and shareware, available on the Internet itself. Most providers include a basic newsreader in their startup software packages for new customers, but these newsreaders are often older shareware versions. Finding a better newsreader is just a matter of logging onto the Net, seeking out one of the many shareware libraries on-line, and taking your pick. (Yahoo! at **http://www.yahoo.com** is a good place to start.)

Another newsreading route for the direct-network or SLIP/PPP user is the "suite" or "Swiss Army Knife" software package. Like the proprietary software of the on-line services, the packages combine several functions (Web browser, mail client, FTP, etc.) in one ornate program and usually contain some sort of newsreader. Unfortunately, these programs tend to suffer from the same woes that afflict the on-line services' software: slowness and substandard features. Still, the all-in-one approach has enormous popular appeal (and consequently is a high priority for software developers), so keep an eye out for improvements in this area. Current versions of the Netscape and Microsoft browsers include newsreaders, which work fairly well but are not the equal of stand-alone applications such as Agent.

One of the most welcome features now becoming popular in well-designed newsreaders is an off-line capability. Rather than forcing the user to read newsgroups while online, a newsreader with this feature allows the user to log on, automatically grab all of the headers (subject/author/date lines) of articles in favorite newsgroups, then log off. The user can leisurely review the headers in each group, pick the ones that sound interesting, and log back on just long enough to allow the newsreader to grab the bodies of the chosen articles. An off-line newsreader can allow you to read articles days or weeks after they are posted (by which time the article itself would probably have expired on the news server and no longer be available).

USENET NEWSGROUPS OF PARTICULAR INTEREST TO READERS

With more than 20,000 Usenet newsgroups to choose from, anyone who attempts to read even just those groups that initially sound interesting will be quickly overwhelmed by the sheer volume of postings. Most people end up subscribing to and regularly reading perhaps seven to ten groups on a regular basis. What follows is a list of a few of my favorites. They don't all relate directly to books or reading, but they're all worth checking out at least occasionally. Many more newsgroups related to books are listed in Chapter 7.

rec.arts.books

This newsgroup is home base for book lovers on the Net. Traffic in the group is brisk, with between fifty and a hundred new postings every day. The discussion topics range from "books set in cold locations—recommendations?" to debates over the possibly deleterious effects of "book superstores" such as Barnes & Noble. The only constants in this group seem to be debates about the works of Ayn Rand and censorship. Most important book-related FAQs are periodically posted here.

bit.listserv.literary

Similar to **rec.arts.books** in many ways, this is a Usenet redistribution of an academic e-mail mailing list and may not be available at some sites. The tone here tends to be a bit heavier, more serious and academic, than that in **rec.arts.books**.

misc.writing

Ain't nobody here but us writers . . . by the hundreds. All sorts of writers, from successful freelancers to aspiring novelists to closet journal keepers, check in here to swap tips on writing, agents, contracts, and copyright law. If you want to be a writer but lack confidence, this is the place to come; probably the most supportive folks on the planet hang out here.

alt.usage.english

Ever wonder where the word *posh* came from? Unsure about the placement of a period with quotation marks? Can't seem to remember what a participle is? Stay up late at night wondering what people in different countries call the strip of grass in the middle of a highway? Here you'll find the answers, along with extended debates on nearly every conceivable issue of English language usage. A high-traffic group, **alt.usage.english** also boasts an extensive and fascinating FAQ updated and posted monthly.

alt.folklore.urban

Is someone in your office collecting soda can pop-tops for a fund to buy a kidney dialysis machine? Is your best friend encouraging you to send hundreds of get-well cards to a sick boy in England so the lad can get into the *Guinness Book of World Records*? Did a friend of a friend bite into a frog lurking in her taco at a fast-food restaurant? Get thee to **alt.folklore.urban** (also known as

AFU), where the mythology of modern life meets its debunkers. One of the more popular groups on Usenet, AFU is home to some of the smartest and funniest regulars on the Net, but they don't suffer fools gladly, so be sure to read the FAQ before posting.

There's also a moderated and thus more "serious" relative of **alt.folklore.urban**, called **alt.folklore.suburban** (the "suburban" connoting a subsidiary relationship to the "urban" group, not a fixation on lawn furniture), where the discussion is governed by the tastes of the moderator. Whether exploding poodles and bizarre suicides really deserve this level of serious discussion, of course, is open to question.

alt.folklore.ghost-stories

All ghost stories, all the time—a sort of twenty-four-hour spook channel on the Net. Here you'll find personal accounts of encounters with somewhat transparent former relatives. It's guaranteed to give even hardened skeptics the wimwams.

alt.humor.best-of-usenet

The funniest messages from the Usenet are helpfully reposted here for your convenience. The quality varies but every so often a true not-to-be-missed classic (such as the famous "Microsoft Buys Catholic Church" announcement) crops up.

soc.history.what-if

What if the Japanese had won World War II? What if President Kennedy hadn't been assassinated? What if Bill Gates hadn't been born, or had been born a girl, or born a goldfish? Welcome to the wonderful world of what if, where hypotheticals flourish and you can let your urge to speculate off the leash and watch it run barking into the woods. Most of the discussion here centers on wars, revolutions, and other cataclysmic events, not surprisingly, but at least the history lessons are never dull. Relentlessly strange, but not dull.

alt.conspiracy

Not a group that anyone should read too closely, but an occasional visit will make you feel rock-solid sane in comparison to some of the folks who hang out here. Mysterious black helicopters, alien abductions, and Microsoft's plans for world domination are all fodder for the nut mill. Most likely the only group on the Net where a thread entitled "The Hollow Earth Theory Is Probably a Hoax" (*probably?*) would prompt a string of serious replies.

alt.politics.correct

Put out that cigarette and pay attention, fascist dog. If you happen to be suffering from low blood pressure, this newsgroup is just the ticket. Left and Right unite in a nonstop paranoid mud-wrestling marathon. This newsgroup features extended debates on Rush Limbaugh's parentage and is best in small doses—just reading the subject lines in this group is enough to tick off most people.

alt.fan.cecil-adams

This is a newsgroup devoted to discussing "The Straight Dope," a syndicated newspaper column that answers such age-old questions as "Where are all the baby pigeons?" and "Why do monopolies bother to advertise?" This is a remarkably civil group, homey and pleasant to read.

comp.internet.net-happenings

Lo and behold, here's a newsgroup that actually contains news. It's one of the best ways to stay abreast of new developments on the Net, especially new mailing lists, e-zines, and Web sites. This is a high-traffic, one-way group (no posting except by the moderator, an incredibly hardworking fellow named Gleason Sackman).

humanities.lit.authors.shakespeare

This is one of the first groups established in a new "humanities" hierarchy. This is a relatively low-traffic group at the moment, but it will probably take off as more sites begin to carry such groups. Besides, if Anne Rice gets a newsgroup, surely there's room for the Bard.

news.newusers.questions

If you're new to the Net, this is the place to ask nearly any question. If you've been around for a while, it's always nice to stop by and answer a few questions. Besides, you'll probably learn something useful yourself.

alt.society.neutopia

Doctress Neutopia (also known as Libby Hubbard) is a sometime graduate student at the University of Massachusetts and author of a (choose one) (a) charmingly idealistic, (b) fundamentally impractical, or (c) clearly demented theory of how to build a new utopian ("Neutopian") society. It's a very long story. This newsgroup not only provides the good Doctress a platform for her, um, pronouncements, but gives her beer-swilling nemeses (known as the Monster Truck Neutopians) a place to post their recipes for barbecue sauce. This group definitely wins the Down-the-Rabbit-Hole Award and has to be read to be believed.

Finding Information on Usenet

Just because Usenet doesn't contain very much "hard news" doesn't mean it can't be an extremely useful source of information. Newsgroups devoted to a particular topic are some of the best sources of information on that topic, since, by definition, the "regulars" in a given group are passionately interested in the topic of the group. On occasion, I have found excellent information about dictionaries of rhyming slang in **alt.usage.english**, helpful explanations of some of the more arcane rituals of the English ruling class in **alt.fan.wodehouse**, and a source for a biography of the Irish humorist Flann O'Brien in **rec.arts.books**. Most regulars in a given group are eager to answer questions about the group's topic (provided that you have checked the group's FAQ for the answer first—no one enjoys answering the same questions over and over).

One caveat: Take everything you read on Usenet with several grains of salt. Chances are that you'll receive more than one reply to any question you post, and it's up to you to decide whom, if anyone, to trust. *Never rely on Usenet for answers to medical, legal, or financial questions,* and be very skeptical about any advice regarding computers that may be offered.

With that in mind, the trick is to find the proper group in which to ask your question. You could scroll through a list of all 20,000-plus newsgroups, if you have the patience, and take a stab at the more likely groups. Or you could zip over to *The Liszt of Newsgroups* page (yes, it's a silly pun) on the World Wide Web at **http://www.liszt.com**. Just enter the topic you're searching for, click on the button, and in a moment a sophisticated search engine will present you with a list of newsgroups meeting your criteria. If you're using Netscape or another browser with an integrated newsreading feature, clicking on the name of a newsgroup will take you right there and you can begin your reading at once. *The Liszt of Newsgroups* page, by the way, is linked to another page called *The Liszt of Lists* (somebody out there really likes that pun), where you can run the same sort of search to find the names and addresses of mailing lists on a given subject.

Another way to search Usenet is offered by *The Deja News Search Page* (yes, yet another corny pun) at **http://www.dejanews.com**. Here you simply type in a word or words to search for, hit the button, and wait for the search engine to present you with a list of articles, fetched from every group on Usenet, containing those words. You can also customize your search by date, number of results, or other criterion. One interesting (and mildly Orwellian) use of the Deja News service is to search for postings by a particular person—the search engine will show you every posting by that person in every group over the last few months.

STARTING A USENET NEWSGROUP

So you've sifted through all 20,000-plus Usenet newsgroups and discovered that, as unbelievable as it seems, there is no group devoted to the work of your favorite author. No **alt.fan.flann-obrien**! No **alt.fan.sj-perelman**! No **alt.fan.winthrop-fortescue**! (Who?) In any case, it's an outrage, and it's up to you to rectify the oversight. What to do? Simple: start the newsgroup yourself.

Starting a Usenet newsgroup may seem to be an awesome undertaking (after all, you're talking about altering the very structure of the global Internet itself), but it really isn't that difficult. I've done it myself: in 1996, I started a newsgroup called **alt.fan.word-detective** to provide readers of my newspaper column with a place to discuss my columns and post questions about word origins. In practical terms, starting an alt. newsgroup is much easier than starting a newsgroup in one of the top-level hierarchies, but there are still a few tricks to it. Fortunately, as is the case with most questions one might have about how the Net works, there is a handy FAQ on the subject. To receive the FAQ, just send an e-mail message to **mail-server@rtfm.mit.edu**, with the following text in the body of the message:

send usenet/alt.config/So_You_Want_to_Create_an_Alt_Newsgroup

(be sure to include those funny-looking underscored spaces between the words—use shift-hyphen on your keyboard). You will then receive by return e-mail a three-part FAQ that explains the process in detail. You can also read the FAQ on a Web page at **http://www.math.psu.edu/barr/alt-creation-guide.html**.

Your first step in creating an alt. group should be to read the above FAQ, but just to whet your appetite (and to prove that it really isn't that difficult), here's a brief rundown of the process. Your next step is to post a proposal for your new group in the **alt.config** newsgroup (which is where news administrators, the folks who run the Usenet news servers at each site on the Net, hang out). Your proposal should be short and to the point, explaining why your group is necessary or desirable, why your subject isn't covered by existing groups, and so on. By the way, it's a good idea to read **alt.config** for at least a few weeks before you post your proposal, by which time you'll have a far better understanding of what to put in your proposal.

Once you've posted your proposal to **alt.config**, sit back and relax for a few weeks while comments on your idea roll in from other Net users. The real aim of this process is not to debate the virtues of Winthrop Fortescue as an author, but rather to demonstrate to the news administrators (who are looking over your shoulder, remember) that you're not a flake and that there is genuine public interest in your fledgling group. If public reaction to your idea in **alt.config** is generally positive, you're on your way.

Now it's time to ask the news administrator at your own site to issue the special "control message" to the Usenet network that will actually create your newsgroup. If for some reason you can't reach your own news administrator, you can always ask someone in **alt.config** itself to issue the control message. In fact, there's actually no reason why you can't issue the control message yourself (as I did when I started my **alt.fan.word-detective** newsgroup). You will need to become very familiar with how your newsreader software works, and follow the instructions in the aforementioned FAQ to the letter, but it really only takes about fifteen minutes to issue the control message and create an alt. group.

Once the control message is issued, the die is cast—either news administrators at other sites on the Net will decide to honor the control message and carry your group or they won't (and some may carry it while others may not). If you've come up with a good idea for a newsgroup and familiarized news administrators with your idea by way of a discussion in **alt.config**, the chances that your newsgroup will be carried by news servers around the world are quite good.

Don't be put off by the challenge of your undertaking; after all, someone recently created a newsgroup called **alt.cows.are.nice**, so it can't be that hard, can it? In the words of the FAQ, "There are no Guidelines or Rules for creating alt. groups. There is no one 'in charge' of the alt. hierarchy. The key to creating a successful alt. newsgroup depends only on convincing the thousands of news administrators across the globe to carry your newsgroup." Piece of cake. After all, nobody doesn't like Winthrop Fortescue, right?

THE DOWNSIDE OF USENET

Although Usenet newsgroups are by far the most popular venue for discussion on the Internet, Usenet has one big problem—"spam." The conventions of Usenet that were adopted in its early days to keep discussions on track and uninterrupted have been increasingly ignored and subverted in recent years. A deluge of spam (commercial advertising messages) has inundated nearly every one of the 20,000-plus Usenet groups over the last two years, in many cases drowning out on-topic conversations and making reading Usenet an intensely frustrating experience. While a new generation of Usenet newsreaders has emerged equipped with filtering features designed to defeat this onslaught of spam, the effectiveness of such filters has been limited by the very virtues of Usenet that originally attracted so many Net users—its openness and lack of central authority. Spammers switch their Internet addresses constantly, and even the most vigilant software cannot filter out a poster's address until that person pops his or her head up by posting spam, by which time it is, by definition, too late to act effectively.

There may yet prove to be a practical solution to the problem of spamming on Usenet. Every on-line service and ISP on the Net may agree to bar spammers from establishing new accounts, or maybe spam will die a natural death over time as more and more spammers discover that millions *cannot* be made by annoying people on-line. It's probable that enlightened service providers hold the only real hope of saving Usenet. There is currently an attempt underway to establish a completely new "parallel" Usenet hierarchy of newsgroups with the prefix "net" (**net.history**, **net.media**, etc.) as a means of wresting control of Usenet from spammers and their ilk. The "net" groups will allow posting only from "sound sites" that vigorously enforce antispamming rules—the equivalent of each group having a "bouncer." Whether the new spam-free "net" newsgroups succeed or not will, unfortunately, probably determine whether Usenet has any real future at all.

WEB-BASED CONFERENCING SYSTEMS AND DISCUSSION GROUPS

Given the problems that have developed in the Usenet newsgroups over the last few years, it's not surprising that many Net users interested in books, literature, and civilized discussion have "bailed out" of Usenet and no longer participate in newsgroup discussions. The good news is that many of the Net's book lovers have migrated to new forums for discussion that are (so far, at least) largely immune to the problems of spamming and incivility that have plagued Usenet. Web-based discussion groups devoted to books and literature have sprung up all over the Net in the past few years.

Web-based discussion groups have two major advantages over Usenet that make them appealing to both Net neophytes and on-line veterans. First (and for many users, foremost), these systems work within your Web browser—no separate software is needed. Messages appear as plain text on your screen, and you can post your own comments simply by typing into a box on a Web page. Navigation between messages and topics is usually simply a matter of clicking your mouse on a "forward" or "back" arrow graphic on the page. Most Web discussion groups also have built-in directories of topics that allow you to jump to the ones you're interested in very easily.

Second, almost all Web discussion groups are "moderated" to some extent. This simply means that someone at the Web site is paying attention to the discussion group—not to limit discussion or censor participants, but to make sure that participants stick to the general topic and refrain from antisocial behavior. This simple practice has made all the difference in Web discussion groups, as opposed to "free for all" Usenet groups. Comments posted in Web discussion groups are much more civil, intelligent, and productive than those you'll find on Usenet today. You won't find any "Get Rich Quick!" postings or pointless "flame wars" in Web discussion groups.

As you might expect, new Web forums and discussion groups are appearing almost daily, but those listed below will give you a good place to start. All of these forums are absolutely free and open to all Net users, although in most cases you will have to go through a short registration process to be able to participate. Some of these discussion groups require that you be using a recent version of either Microsoft Internet Explorer or Netscape software, so you may need to update your browser if you're using an older version. (Note to America Online users: Your AOL software already contains a recent version of Internet Explorer, so you're all set.)

Atlantic Monthly Post & Riposte Discussions of the arts, politics, and society, closely tied to the magazine's contents.
http://www.theatlantic.com/atlantic/pr/index.htm

Barnes and Noble Book Forum Discussions on a wide variety of literary topics (including such appropriate subjects as "Why books cost so much").
http://www.barnesandnoble.com/

Book Stacks Book Forums Post your opinions on topics ranging from the classic mysteries of Agatha Christie to the latest choice for Oprah's Book Club.
http://www.books.com/

Cafe Utne Hosted by *The Utne Reader*. Fascinating discussions on a wide range of literature.
http://www.utne.com/cafe/index.html

New York Times Book Review Round Table Forum *The New York Times* has put its pacesetting *Book Review* online at last, and it serves as a springboard for the hundreds of lively discussions in this forum.
http://forums.nytimes.com/books/forums/

Poets and Writers Online Speakeasy Lively discussions about the art and business of writing from one of the premier writers magazines.
http://www.pw.org/speak.htm

Salon Tabletalk Hosted by *Salon*, one of the best of the on-line magazines of art and culture. A new feature, "Salon Classics," brings contemporary authors on-line to discuss classic literature with participants (Erica Jong discussing *Madame Bovary*, for instance).
http://tabletalk.salon1999.com/webx

SeniorNet You don't have to be a "senior" to participate in the hundreds of book-related discussions here. Sections on mystery, adventure, classics, and other genres.
http://www.seniornet.com/

Washington Post Talk Central Hundreds of discussions in the "Books and More" area. There's also an on-line book club where readers read and discuss one book together.
http://www.washingtonpost.com/wp-srv/talk/front.htm

Chapter 5

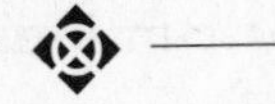

Mailing Lists: News and Views in Your E-Mailbox

Of all the features of the Internet, probably the most versatile is e-mail, or electronic mail. The ability to send messages to another person thousands of miles away, almost instantaneously and without the need for stamps or a trip to the mailbox, is inarguably nifty. There have been many commentaries written on the social impact of the advent of e-mail—whether it sounds the death knell of "real" handwritten correspondence or whether the inherently ephemeral nature of e-mail means that it is taken less seriously than "hard copy" mail. One thing is certain: The ease of sending and receiving e-mail makes maintaining electronic correspondence so quick and painless that even newcomers to the Net often find themselves developing e-mail pen pals. Such relationships are not necessarily as ephemeral as the medium would lead some to believe;

stories abound of couples who have met, courted, and become engaged to be married, all via e-mail.

There are many ways to develop a group of e-mail pen pals—responding via e-mail directly to the author of a post in a Usenet newsgroup that you find insightful or clever, for instance, will usually garner at least a reply. There is even a Usenet newsgroup (**soc.penpals**) devoted entirely to matching likely Net pen pals, and a posting to that group stating one's interest ("book lover looking for same") is likely to produce a few candidates.

There is, however, an easier way to develop an e-mail correspondence with Net users who share your particular interest—often, in fact, with hundreds or thousands of like-minded people, all at one fell swoop. Joining an Internet mailing list will instantly make you part of an on-line community of people who share your passion, whether it is gardening, ham radio, raising prizewinning gerbils or, of course, books and reading. As is the case with many aspects of the Net, exact figures are hard to come by, but there are more than 70,000 mailing lists operating on the Net and new ones spring up nearly every day.

Internet mailing lists were originally developed in the early days of the Net as a way for researchers to share results and participate in discussions with colleagues in their fields. Because participating in a mailing list requires only some sort of Net e-mail connection, it is possible to participate in a mailing list even if you lack any other sort of Internet access, such as Usenet or the Web.

Participating in a mailing list is simplicity incarnate. Once you join or subscribe to a given list, you will receive all e-mail messages sent to that list by other members. If you wish to make a contribution to the list, you simply send your e-mail message to the list address, and everyone else on the list will automatically receive your posting as an e-mail message.

The benefits of subscribing to a list are numerous. You'll be joining a community of people who share your specific interest, so your discussions will not be interrupted (as they often are on Usenet) by off-topic postings or annoying commercial advertisements. Because postings to the list come to you as e-mail messages, you'll have a complete, permanent record of what was said and not run the risk (as on Usenet) of missing part of a discussion if you don't tune in for a few days. You can always wait a day or two to open your e-mail, after all.

But perhaps the best aspect of participating in a mailing list is the remarkable sense of community that lists inspire. Because a mailing list is made up of people who have taken the time to join it (as opposed to merely wandering into a Usenet newsgroup by chance), list members often get to know each other fairly well, and the semi-private nature of the list encourages a more personal, trusting atmosphere than Usenet does. The sense of continuity encouraged by a list (many lists have lasted for more than ten years) also lends both coherence and seriousness to discussions that you simply won't find on the open Net.

Because mailing lists were originally an academic invention, they offer particular attractions for users interested in books and reading. A mailing list devoted to Jane Austen, for instance, is likely to unite everyday fans of

Austen with serious academic students of her work. The discussions found on mailing lists devoted to literature often attain a depth of intellectual sophistication unknown on the rest of the Internet or, for that matter, in any other mass medium. At the same time, most lists manage to avoid a didactic tone, perhaps because participation is entirely voluntary, fueled by a genuine interest in the topic.

SUBSCRIBING TO A MAILING LIST

The key to every Net mailing list is the automatic software program called a "listserver" that runs the list, usually a program called "Listserv," "Listproc," or "Majordomo." The program runs on a central computer (often at a university), receives all messages sent to the list, and redistributes them to the other participants. Many listservers also archive, or keep a permanent transcript of, the contents of the list, and all listservers respond to commands that allow users to choose the form in which they receive the list (as separate messages or as a daily digest of messages).

Every mailing list has two addresses, and keeping the two straight is extremely important. One is the *listserver address*. This is the address of the central computer to which you send messages (called "user commands") to join the list, quit the list, or change your user options. The other address is the address of the list itself (the *list address*). This is where you should send messages that you want forwarded to the other subscribers of the list. *Never, never, send user commands to the list address.* If you do, everyone who subscribes to the list will receive your commands and be very annoyed, but the listserver program itself will remain completely unaware of your wishes. There are few things more annoying to list participants than being deluged by repeated misdirected user commands from a clueless newcomer.

To join a list, send an e-mail message to the listserver address of the specific listserver. The message to join must be in a particular format, because it is being read by a computer, not a person. Leave the subject line of the message blank, and in the body of the message put "subscribe *listname your personal name*." If you're joining a Majordomo list, leave off your name entirely. Be sure to use your personal name, not your e-mail address (the listserver will get your e-mail address from the header information on the message, so that's no problem). If you normally use a programmed signature on your e-mail messages, be sure to turn it off for this message, or you'll get an alarming error report from an irate listserver program by return e-mail.

There are a few (usually low-volume) lists that are run, not by listservers, but by actual human beings. In the case of these lists, just write directly to the list maintainer (called the "list owner") and ask to be added to the list.

FINDING A LIST TO JOIN

Although joining a list is a simple matter of sending an e-mail message to the listserver, finding a list you'd like to join is often a bit more difficult. As is the case with

Usenet, there is no "Mailing List Central" running the show, and starting a list really only requires the cooperation of someone who owns a computer running a listserver program. Consequently, new lists appear frequently and there is no absolutely complete and reliable listing of what lists are available. On the other hand, there are a number of ways to find lists on a given subject.

The first step is to check Chapter 7 of this book, where you'll find many mailing lists indexed along with other Internet resources. If you're interested in finding a list not included there, check the "Search the List of Lists" Web page at **http://catalog.com/vivian/interest-group-search.html**. This page searches the entire master list of mailing lists by any keyword you choose and will return a list of candidates, with a complete description of each list and subscription information.

Another way to track down lists on a particular subject is to check an exhaustive compilation maintained by Stephanie De Silva called *Publicly Accessible Mailing Lists* (PAML). PAML is available several ways on the Net: It is periodically posted in a multipart format to the Usenet newsgroups **news.answers** and **news.announce.newusers**, and it is also available on Web pages at **http://www.cis.ohio-state.edu/text/faq/usenet/mail/mailing-lists/top.html** or **http://www.neosoft.com/internet/paml**.

Another good source of list information is at **http://www.tile.Net/tile/listserv**. The only drawback here is that it includes only lists running on Listserv software (and not Majordomo lists, for example). Yet another source is Nova Southeastern University's E-Mail Discussion Group page at **http://www.nova.edu/Inter-Links/**

listserv.html. This page also offers help files containing excellent background information on joining and working with mailing lists.

If you're looking for a list on an academic subject, you'll probably want to check the *Directory of Scholarly Electronic Conferences*, produced by Diane Kovacs and the Directory Team at the Kent State University Libraries. The Directory is an exhaustive multipart catalog of lists covering major subjects. It is available via e-mail by sending the message "get acadlist.readme" to **listserv@kentvm.kent.edu**. You will receive return e-mail listing available subject files, which you can then fetch via e-mail with the appropriate "get" command.

Since there are new lists being created all the time, you'll need a way to keep up with them. The easiest way is to check the Usenet newsgroup **news.lists**, where announcements of new lists are posted. Another method is to subscribe to the *Net-Happenings* e-mail newsletter produced by Gleason Sackman, available by sending the command "subscribe Net-happenings" (you don't need to include your name) to **majordomo@dsmail.internic.Net.** You'll receive daily listings, not just of new lists, but of almost everything new on the Net as a whole. If you prefer to receive *Net-Happenings* in digest form (which I highly recommend), just send the message "subscribe Net-happenings-digest" to the same address. Mr. Sackman's announcements are also posted to the Usenet newsgroup **comp.internet.net-happenings**.

There is also a mailing list dealing with announcements of new lists, available by sending the request "subscribe new-list" to **listserv@vm1.Nodak.Edu**. Unless you're absolutely certain that you want to subscribe to a given list, it might be a good idea to ask for information about the list before you actually sign up. To do so, just send the message "info *listname your name*" to the list server instead of "subscribe *listname your name.*" You'll then receive a file describing the list that will give you a better idea of what you're getting into.

Participating in a Mailing List

After you join a list, you'll probably begin receiving mail from the list within a day or two. You'll also receive an automatic confirmation message sent by the listserver, letting you know that your "subscribe" request was understood and that you are, in fact, now part of the list. *Save this message—it is extremely important.* It will tell you how to go about setting various list options, how to search the archives of the list if they exist, how to "pause" the list so you don't find 600 messages waiting when you get back from vacation, and how to quit the list. If you subscribe to more than one list, it's probably worth your time to create a special directory in your e-mail program for storing these messages. Even automated lists, by the way, have a human owner (listed in the confirmation message) whom you can contact in an emergency.

Read whatever confirmation message you get from the list very carefully—in many cases you must reply to the message within a day or two with a simple pro forma message to verify your e-mail address and to affirm your desire to join the list. If you do not reply, you will not be added to the list. List administrators have found it necessary to adopt this method of verification to prevent "net kooks" from subscribing the objects of their wrath (journalists in particular, for some reason) to 800 mailing lists by forging their e-mail addresses.

Remember that in joining a list you're actually joining an on-line community that may have existed for years before your arrival, so good manners require that you spend a bit of time reading the messages among list members before adding your two cents' worth. Once you've developed a feel for the group, go ahead and jump right in. In most cases, replying to a message from someone on the list is simply a matter of hitting the "reply" button in your e-mail program—the listserver program will automatically send copies of your message to everyone on the list. If you want to conduct a private correspondence with someone on the list, however, you'll have to make sure that you type their personal address, not the list address, into the "to" field of your reply. And, of course, if you ever decide to quit the list, you'll have to dig out that "welcome" message you received when you joined to find the proper address to which you should send your "quit" message.

MAILING LISTS AND YOUR SANITY

It may seem unlikely that, having found and joined a list devoted to your favorite subject, you would ever wish to leave it, but, trust me, there's a chance you will. Although Internet mailing lists are a wonderful invention, there are two main problems with many lists, and in some cases they become so severe that users bail out in frustration.

The first problem is volume. A busy list can generate hundreds of postings per week, and no matter how much you enjoy talking about the subject, there are still only twenty-four hours in a day and not enough time to read all of those messages. You may reach a point at which opening your e-mail program in the morning and finding sixty messages waiting to be read is simply too much to bear. Some lists give you the option of receiving the list in daily or weekly digest form, which may solve the problem for you (or make it easier to ignore, at least). Because of the volume generated by some lists, it's important to subscribe to lists one at a time, waiting for a week or so in order to gauge the traffic level of the new list before subscribing to another. Never subscribe to two or three lists on the same day. I've done it myself, and it's not a pretty sight when you start getting 200 messages every day.

The second problem with some lists is "topic drift": instead of talking about the avowed subject, participants drift into chatting about their children, their cats, or the movies they saw recently. You may find this sort of thing either charming or infuriating. Whether a given list drifts too far from its topic or not is a matter of taste, of course, but a good list will stick fairly close to the subject.

Chapter 6

How to Be Your Own Publisher: Putting Yourself On-line

A writer, someone once observed, is simply a reader moved by admiration to emulation. Just as there are few writers who are not also passionate readers, so there are few readers who have not at least dreamed of finding an audience for their creative endeavors. If you've ever yearned for a way to bring your poetry or prose to the public, your ship has arrived. The Internet is the largest self-publishing experiment in history. Think of it: The Internet "publishes" every day of the year; it is, for the most part, unedited and uncensored; and it has a global readership of between 30 million and 50 million people (at least a few hundred of whom are bound to recognize that poem you wrote to your cat as the masterpiece that it is). There are several ways to publish your own work or to find someone else to publish it on the Internet, all of which are open to anyone with a computer and Internet access. And, of course, there's always the chance that a major publisher will see your work on-line and offer you a huge contract and make your book an instant bestseller and pretty soon you'll be starring in a TV movie based on that poem you wrote to your cat. Hey, it's not impossible.

POSTING YOUR WORK ON USENET

Probably the easiest way to publish your own work on the Net is simply to post it to one of the Usenet newsgroups designed for just that purpose:

alt.prose	postings of original writings, both fiction and nonfiction
rec.arts.prose	short works of prose fiction and follow-up discussion
rec.arts.poems	for the posting of poems

There is also a newsgroup called **alt.prose.d**, where the "d" stands for "discussion," but a good deal of discussion takes place in **alt.prose** itself. It also is possible to post your writings in **alt.etext**, although that group tends to concentrate on electronic newsletters, e-zines (electronic magazines), and news of classic texts converted to digital form by groups such as Project Gutenberg.

The advantage of posting in one of these Usenet newsgroups is that you'll get instant exposure to a broad audience, and probably at least some public reaction to your work in the form of follow-up postings to your original message. The disadvantage of this method is that Usenet postings are by their very nature ephemeral, and your work will evaporate from most news servers within a few days. Publishing your work this way is a bit like writing it in chalk on the sidewalk: lots of people will see it if they happen to be passing by, but it will never end up in the Library of Congress. Still, it's a good way to start, and, assuming that public reaction to what you write is positive, it may give you just the encouragement you need to seek a higher-profile outlet for your work.

Electronic Literary Journals and E-zines

A way to see your work in print in a somewhat more prestigious (and more permanent) venue is to submit it to one of the hundreds of electronic journals and e-zines on the Internet. Going this route is not exactly self-publishing, since even the most informal e-zine has someone who acts as editor and chooses what to publish. But the good news is that, because there are so many new electronic publications on the Net (and more popping up every day), most on-line journals are actively seeking contributions from writers, so the chances of your work being accepted by one or more are actually quite good.

Most of the Net literary journals and e-zines listed in Chapter 7 accept submissions, and many of them post writers' guidelines on their home pages. Your first step should be to browse the ranks of on-line publications and pick a few that you are interested in submitting your work to; then contact the editors and briefly describe your work, asking how to submit it for consideration. Don't expect an immediate reply; many of the smaller e-zines are run by people with day jobs and busy lives. But don't worry—sooner or later you'll be able to tell your friends to check out your work at **http://www.bigtime.com**.

If you need further encouragement, keep in mind that some of these electronic journals are on-line outposts of respected print journals, so by being published on-line, you may be getting a foot in the door of the off-line publishing world.

STARTING YOUR OWN ELECTRONIC NEWSLETTER

If you really feel that you have a lot to say that isn't being said elsewhere on the Internet, you may want to consider starting your own electronic newsletter. There are thousands of such newsletters on the Net, on just as many topics, delivering news and views on everything from mystery fiction (see *The ClueLass Homepage* at **http://www.slip.net/~cluelass/** for information) to miraculous encounters with angels (see **http://www.netangel.com/** for details), many with thousands of subscribers. If you'd like to get a sense of what's out there on the Net, just search at Yahoo! **(http://www.yahoo.com)** under the word *newsletter*—the list you'll get goes on forever.

The secret of such newsletters' success is simplicity; a newsletter, after all, is just a glorified e-mail message sent to each subscriber. Each month, or week, or whatever, the newsletter's editor puts together a text file and mails it to the subscribers, just the way you'd send an e-mail message to your aunt.

E-mail newsletters can be modest or ambitious, but you're probably better off starting simple. Keep it short: less than 2,000 words is a good idea, especially because some e-mail programs that your subscribers may be using have difficulty accepting longer messages. Whether you plan to charge money for your newsletter is, of course, up to you, but keep in mind that the vast majority of Internet newsletters are free.

Once you have your newsletter ready to go, the next step is to announce it. The easiest way to do this is to post a brief announcement in the Usenet newsgroups to which your newsletter is most relevant. If your newsletter is about Scandinavian detective fiction, for instance, post your announcement to **rec.arts.mystery** as well as **rec.arts.books**. *Do not post the newsletter itself*, tempting as that may be. If you post the whole thing, you may inadvertently force anyone being charged by the minute for Internet access to pay to download your newsletter whether they're interested in it or not, which is hardly the way to win friends on the Net.

You should also announce your newsletter in the *Net-Happenings* mailing list. The easiest way to do this is via the *Net-Happenings* Web site (**http://www.mid.net**), which features a handy submittal form you can fill out on the spot and explains exactly how to word your announcement.

Once your announcement is out on the Net, you'll start to get requests for your newsletter from people who want to subscribe. The important thing to do now is to save the return address from each of these messages—in most cases, that's where you'll be sending your newsletter. A good e-mail program, such as Eudora (available for both PCs and Macs), will allow you to extract the sender address from any mail you receive, but if you're using an on-line service's e-mail software, you may have to manually cut and paste the address into your e-mail address book. A good e-mail program will also allow you to create groups of addresses, which can make sending out your newsletter much simpler: just add new subscribers to a newsletter address group as they join, and when it's time to publish, send your newsletter to the entire group in one simple step. If your e-mail program won't allow you to create this kind of group, it may at least allow you to create separate folders within your address book, so at least subscribers' addresses won't get mixed in with those of anyone else you happen to have. One helpful hint that I myself learned the hard way: Make sure that whatever e-mail program you use allows you to address your list members as "BCC" (meaning "Blind Carbon Copy," a quaint holdover in terminology from the days of typewriters and carbon paper). Sending mail BCC prevents every recipient from seeing the e-mail address of every other recipient—a courtesy that your subscribers will (trust me on this) appreciate.

Mailing your newsletter yourself is the best way to start out, but once your creation becomes popular (more than a hundred subscribers or so), you'll probably find that dealing with subscription requests and mailing hundreds of copies of your newsletter becomes unmanageable. When you reach this point, you may want to look into converting your newsletter to a mailing list newsletter running on a Listserv or Majordomo computer program, which will manage the day-to-day details (see Chapter 5 for an explanation of how these programs work). Since most of these listserver programs are run on large computers at universities and other institutions, you'll probably have to find someone willing to give you space on their listserver. Your first step in finding such space is the logical one: Ask your subscribers. There's a good chance they'll know someone who can help. You can also post a query in the Usenet newsgroups where you first announced your newsletter. This should do the trick, but if all else fails, drop a note to the editor of a similar newsletter that is distributed as a mailing list (another mystery newsletter, for example), and you're almost certain to get good advice.

Publishing Yourself on the World Wide Web

Judging by the recent explosion in the number of aspiring writers' and poets' home pages on the World Wide Web, a great untapped reservoir of creative energy has finally found its outlet. Personal Web pages, stored in individual users' home directories on Web servers maintained by access providers, now number in the tens of thousands. They range from simple "here I am and here's a picture of my cat" pages to some of the most valuable and entertaining sites on the Web. Many of the resources listed in this book, in fact, began as personal home pages and now receive thousands of "hits," or visitors, every day.

If you've always dreamed of finding a place to publish your own writing, you've probably realized by now that a personal Web page might just be the answer to your prayers, an easy way to bring your work directly to a worldwide audience numbering in the tens of millions.

What can you put on your Web page? Anything your heart desires—poems or essays, favorite cookie recipes, that novel you started to write in college, the story of your family. If it's yours and it's legal, you can put it on the Web page. You can't include someone else's copyrighted material, however, but you're free to add links to any other resource on the Net. If you think the Shakespeare Web (**http://www.shakespeare.com/**), for example, is especially neat, you can put a link on your page that will take your visitors directly there with just a mouse click.

What's Behind That Web Page?

Looking at some of the visually striking personal pages on the Web, you'd never guess the big secret about Web sites, which is that creating one really isn't that hard. In fact, it's remarkably simple (honest!) and if you have a word processing program, some sort of Internet connection, and a basic familiarity with saving and moving files, you're already halfway there.

Every Web page you see on your screen is actually a document, a file similar to one you might work with in a word processing program. But instead of being a WordPerfect or Microsoft Word file, Web pages are in the HTML (hypertext markup language) format. The HTML document itself is in the standard ASCII (plain text) format. What makes it an HTML document is that it is full of what are called "HTML tags," which are formatting codes—simply directions for the browser to follow in displaying the page.

Let's suppose that I'm typing a memo in WordPerfect, and I want a certain paragraph to appear in boldface. I highlight the text and click on "bold," thereby inserting "begin bold" and "end bold" codes at either end of the paragraph, right? Well, if I'm making a Web page and want a paragraph to be in boldface, I just insert a tag that says "<bold>" at the beginning and one that says "</bold>" at the end. That's it—I told you it was simple. As a matter of fact, the folks who invented HTML had to keep it simple, because HTML had to be able to work on any sort of computer, not just one system.

There are many more codes than just "<bold>" in HTML, of course, but the principle for all of them is the same. There are simple codes for headline styles, slightly more complicated codes for inserting pictures onto the page, codes for links to other pages, and codes that will let visitors to your page send you e-mail with just a click of their mouse. But all of them are ultimately straightforward and logical.

Learning HTML

The best way to learn HTML and all the other things you'll need to know in order to create a "killer home page" is to read one of the many books available on the subject. One book I'd strongly recommend is *Teach Yourself Web Publishing With HTML in 14 Days* (Laura Lemay, Sams Publishing Co., 1997, $41.99): a very lucid and logical tutorial. And it works—I learned HTML from a previous edition. Laura Lemay, incidentally, is so good at teaching this stuff that she has become a one-woman HTML-teaching empire, with twenty-nine books in print on the topic.

There are, of course, many other good HTML guides on the market. A visit to any large bookstore is likely to turn up at least three or four that strike a good balance between simplicity and depth.

If you're really on a shoestring budget, or just want to dip your toe in HTML before taking the plunge, go to Yahoo! (**http://www.yahoo.com**) and search under "HTML guide." You'll find a dozen or so excellent on-line introductory courses on HTML, and they're all absolutely free.

If you'd like to take a peek at how some of your favorite Web pages were developed, just click on the "View Source" or "View HTML" menu item in your Web browser next time you're on-line, and you'll see the coding. You usually can save the coded text to your own hard drive to study later, which is a great way to pick up HTML coding tricks.

Web Page Construction Tools

It's possible to create a Web page using nothing more than a simple word processing program (as long as it can save documents in ASCII text, which most programs can), but the truth is that typing all those little tags gets very tiresome very quickly. Users of the Microsoft Word and WordPerfect word processing systems have a head start: Current versions of those programs have been upgraded to incorporate HTML editing functions, allowing users to create HTML documents easily.

If you don't use one of those word processing systems, there are several free or nearly free HTML authoring tools available. These programs are basically text editors (they do all their work in ASCII to begin with) with buttons you can click on to insert all the codes you'll ever want to use. The best place to find these programs is on the Net itself—check out the *Jumbo Shareware Archives* at **http://www.jumbo.com**, or simply search Yahoo! at **http://www.yahoo.com** using the search term "HTML editor."

You may be tempted to shell out major money for an HTML editor or Web page production program that promises to make creating a fancy page as easy as "dragging and dropping" page elements and text. These programs, known as "WYSIWYG" (What You See Is What You Get) editors, make their main selling point freedom from the supposedly hideously difficult process of creating your own HTML code. (Programs of this type include Microsoft's Frontpage and Adobe's Page Mill). I would recommend against buying one of these expensive programs for two reasons. First, they are actually awkward and confusing to use—much more so than a simple text-based HTML editing program. The "learning curve" of these programs is quite steep, and you may well give up in frustration long before you ever get your Web page done and up. Second, writing your own HTML really is (honest!) simple and quick, and if you write it yourself, you can modify or "tweak" it any time you choose because you will understand how to do it quickly and simply, without wasting time trying to figure out how to convince a bulky and awkward WYSIWYG program to do it for you.

If you're using one of the major on-line services and you're interested in creating a fairly simple Web page, you're in luck. Each of these services offers the ability to create a personal home page and, even better, an automatic program that you can download from the service itself to handle the process for you. The program will lead you through a question-and-answer session to determine just how you want the page to look ("Picture of cat—yes or no?"), then do all the coding and upload the page to the service for you.

Finally, if you don't use one of the major on-line services but you're eager to develop a Web page without learning any HTML at all, there's a free program available that's similar to the automatic programs offered by the on-line services. Called Web Wizard, the program will lead you through a simple question-and-answer session and give you a completed, albeit rudimentary, personal Web page when it's done. Web Wizard is available at **http://www.halcyon.com/artamedia/webwizard/**.

Once you've completed your Web page, it's a good idea to test it by looking at it with a Web browser while the page is still on the hard drive of your home computer; it's much easier to fix any glitches at this stage than after the page is up and running on the Web. Most browsers will allow you to open and view a local file on your hard drive (look in the "File" menu of your browser), although you may have to sign onto your Internet access provider, open the browser, then sign off to get the browser running. Once you have your page displayed in the browser, be sure to carefully proofread the text.

Nothing will turn off visitors to your page more than careless typographical errors. If you've included links to other places on the Web, sign on to your access provider, load your page from the hard drive, and click on those links to make sure that they actually work and will take your visitors where you want them to go.

Putting Your Page On-line

Once your page is done and checked, your last hurdle is to get it up and running on the Web. This usually isn't difficult, but how you do it will depend on how you access the Net. Most Internet service providers will provide free space on their servers to store pages. They also have developed painless ways for customers to upload and maintain personal Web pages, so all you need to do is ask the customer support folks at your service. You'll probably need to use an FTP program (see Chapter 3) to transfer the files into your home directory. I do it myself every two weeks when I update my home page, and the whole process takes me less than ten minutes each time.

If you're using a major on-line service, you're in luck again: Its Web page creation program will guide you through the steps necessary to upload your page on the service's Web server.

Points to Ponder About Your Web Page

There are a few pitfalls to avoid in designing a Web page. Don't overload it with large or fancy graphics—they take forever to download on a slow link and will only annoy your visitors. The same goes for fancy fonts and background images: Simple is always better on the Web. The Web is littered with pages sporting ornate background images that serve only to obscure their actual content, often making the page's text literally unreadable. Don't do this to your readers, no matter how much you like paisley. I visited hundreds of Web pages in the course of writing this book, and the ones that took forever to load because of huge, pointless graphics or inflicted flashing magenta imagemaps on my tired eyes are not listed in this book.

And again, don't forget to spell-check your page. You want your readers to pay attention to what you've written—not your typographical errors.

Take the time to find out how to make your page visible to visitors using any sort of browser, not just the latest generation of Netscape. Ideally, visitors should have a reason to come visit your page even if they're using a text-only browser such as Lynx and can't see your pretty pictures and fancy designs.

That last consideration brings us back to the question of content and the Web. The only reason for people to come back again and again to your page is the content you put there. If you build it, they will come once, but they'll only come back if there's something interesting. Give folks something to read, on the other hand, and update it often, and you'll be a hit. So much of the Web is a wasteland of computer gimmickry, "cyberpunk" juvenilia, and bad jokes that anything actually readable will win fans in droves.

This means that there is a ready-made audience, potentially in the thousands, for almost anything you've written.

For example, I post my thrice-weekly newspaper column to my Web page (somewhat after it has run in the newspapers that pay for it, of course), and I've gradually built up an audience of more than a thousand regular weekly visitors (it's at **http://www.word-detective.com/**, since you asked). Although I have done no promotion for my page, it has been reviewed and recommended by all sorts of publications, from *USA Today* to *The Jerusalem Post*, and even won the prestigious "Cool Site of the Day" award sponsored by Apple Computer, Inc. and *People* magazine. Best of all, I've discovered that if I'm late in updating my page, I actually get irate e-mail from readers demanding to know where the new columns are. This is enormously gratifying, and although my humble page will never attain the status of the Time Warner or CNN sites, it's nice to know that reading what I write has become part of quite a few folks' weekly routine.

So dust off that old play, or poem, or screenplay, or book review, or write something brand-new, and put it up there on the Web where it belongs.

Chapter 7

On-line Resources for Book Lovers

Compiling a catalog of the Internet, even one focusing on a single topic, is a daunting task. The culprit is the constant, explosive growth of the Internet itself. Like a boisterous child, the Net will simply not sit still to have its picture taken. While the World Wide Web, for example, consisted of just a few hundred sites in late 1993, as of early 1997 there were well over 650,000 Web sites, each of which may house hundreds of pages. As of 1997, more than 17 million computers were connected full-time to the Internet, a number that does not include most personal computers (which are connected to the Net only when they dial in via a phone line). Anyone attempting to round up everything available on the Internet will quickly learn just how frazzled the sorcerer's apprentice felt.

In compiling this list of Internet resources, I've focused

on Net sites that bring a variety of reading resources together in one place, are themselves especially interesting or unusual, or are representative of a particular type of resource. Rather than including the location of every single on-line bookstore or e-text on the Internet, for example, I've listed a few samples and highlighted on-line directories where many more can be found.

Most of the resources noted here are available to anyone with access to the Internet, but I've also included a representative sampling of resources available only on America Online. With more than 7 million users, AOL is by far the most popular on-line service, and many readers will be making their first forays into the on-line world through AOL, so it seems sensible to highlight a few of the notable features available within AOL itself. I've also included a sampling of the more than 250 conferences (discussion groups) available through The WELL, a smaller on-line service of special interest to readers (see Chapter 2).

The list is arranged roughly by genre—romance, mystery, science fiction, and so on—as well as by a few other logical categories. Although I've included FTP and telnet resources, the list is very heavily weighted in favor of World Wide Web sites, as the Web is the most popular, and the most easily accessible, part of today's Internet. The Web also offers the enormous advantage of interconnectivity: Nearly every Web site listed here contains links to dozens, sometimes hundreds, of other Web pages of interest to the book lover. This list, therefore, should be viewed as a collection of starting points, not destinations.

Within many sections of this list you will find Usenet discussion groups and mailing lists related to literature as well as to the particular topic of each section. Many more newsgroups and mailing lists focusing on some of these interest areas (science fiction, for instance) exist than I have included here, but I've chosen the mailing lists and newsgroups specifically dealing with the literature of that particular subject. If you're interested in finding other Usenet newsgroups, visit the Liszt of Newsgroups Web page (**http://www.liszt.com/**), where you'll be able to search for newsgroups by topic. Similarly, a search of the Publicly Accessible Mailing Lists Web page (**http://www.neosoft.com/internet/paml/**) will direct you to other mailing lists devoted to your area of interest.

Detailed instructions for subscribing to mailing lists can be found in Chapter 5. In this chapter, the name or subject of the list is given first, followed by the formal name (what you should call it when sending a subscription or other request to the automatic listserver program that runs the list), then the address of the listserver carrying the list. In almost every case, subscribing is simply a matter of sending an e-mail message to the listserver address (which I have helpfully identified by "**Mail to:**" in each mailing list entry), leaving the subject line blank and the body of the message reading **subscribe listname your name** (e.g., **subscribe DOROTHY-L Bob Bookworm**). If the list address is a Majordomo program (e.g., **majordomo@bowwow.edu**), it's not necessary to include your name in the message.

Equally important information about participating in Usenet newsgroups can be found in Chapter 4.

Every effort has been made to ensure that the addresses of the resources listed here are accurate, but if you should discover that something has become inaccessible or has changed its address, please drop me a note at **netbook@ word-detective.com**, so that it can be corrected in future editions of this book. Similarly, if you feel that I have inexplicably overlooked a great literary site on the Net, please let me know.

Note: Comments on a particular site contained within quotation marks are taken from the site's own description of itself. All other comments are the author's personal opinions. Your mileage may vary.

UNDERSTANDING NAMES AND PLACES ON THE INTERNET

The Internet is a very big place, made up of thousands of computers located all over the world. Because no one really "runs" the Internet, there is no map an explorer can depend on, and no "Directory Assistance" to call for help in finding a particular person or place on the Net. Fortunately, there are several ways to search the Internet, as well as detailed directories by the score.

Every computer on the Internet has a unique address, which (once you find out what it is) makes connecting to computers on the other side of the world as easy as dialing a phone number. In this book I have used the standard format for Internet addresses, known as the uniform resource locator, or URL. Each URL consists of a string of letters or numbers, for example, **http://www.bowwow.com/~fido**.

In each URL, the letters preceding the colon denote the method used to access the site:

http: or hypertext transfer protocol: a site on the World Wide Web

ftp: or file transfer protocol: a file that can be downloaded to your home computer

telnet: a telnet computer that you can log onto

All of these access methods are explained in Chapter 3.

The letters and numbers after the colon, which are always preceded by a double forward slash, identify the specific computer or site to which you'll be connecting. In the example above, "**http**" identifies the resource as a site on the World Wide Web, "**www.bowwow.com**" identifies the specific host computer, and "**/~fido**" identifies the specific directory on that computer's hard drive in which the resource resides. The odd character before "**fido**" in the last part of the address is a tilde (found in the upper left-hand section of most keyboards), which is often used to denote a particular individual's home directory on a computer that may have thousands of users. Occasionally you'll see a URL that includes scored spaces (e.g., **ftp://ftp.neato.com/stuff/neat_stuff.txt**)—just be sure to use the shifted character on the same key as the hyphen.

All the resources mentioned in this book are identified in the standard URL format, in the form **http://www.bowwow.com/~fido**.

In many cases, you won't need to type in the entire URL. In other words, if you're connecting to an FTP site, you won't have to type "**ftp://ftp.rtfm.mit.edu**"—just "**ftp.rtfm.mit.edu**".

Certain Web browsers do require you to type in the

full URL, beginning with "**http:**", in order to tell the browser the type of site to which it's connecting. Other browsers can determine this information automatically, but when in doubt, it doesn't hurt to type the entire address.

If You Have Problems With an Internet Address

Because Internet addresses can be complex, typographical errors in both print and on-line directories are not uncommon. It's also not uncommon for resources on the Net to change their addresses. Sometimes you'll call up a Web page and find a forwarding address, but many times you'll get the dreaded message "Error 404—that file does not exist on this server." (One e-zine on the Web has even waggishly taken "Error 404" as its title [**http://www.cban.com/error404/**].) If you're trying to access a particular site and repeatedly receive only error messages for your efforts, you may be able to reach your goal by cropping the address. If **ftp.neato.com/stuff/neat_stuff.txt** doesn't work, try **ftp.neato.com/stuff/**. This method, when it works, will connect you to the parent directory of the directory or file you were looking for in the first place. From there, you can find the file you want by simply looking through the parent directory. The name of the file may be slightly different from what you had been told, or it may have been moved to a different directory, but if it exists at the site, you'll probably find it with a little poking around.

INTERNET METAPAGES, INDEXES, AND SEARCH ENGINES

While the Internet as a whole is notoriously unorganized, with its best resources often scattered literally all over the globe, finding things on the Net is often quite simple with the aid of the numerous indexes, lists, and search engines available on the Net itself.

General Indexes and Metapages

The following is a selected list of general resource indexes of the Internet. (A metapage is essentially a list of lists.) These sources are probably your best starting points when searching for information on any particular subject. They also make for fascinating browsing even if you're not looking for anything in particular.

Yahoo! It's not just a search engine, it's also probably the best overall index of the Internet, and features a lucid branching-tree directory structure.
http://www.yahoo.com

Clearinghouse for Subject-Oriented Internet Resource Guides No matter what you're looking for on the Net, someone has probably written a guide on how to find it. This is a list of all of those helpful guides.
http://www.clearinghouse.net/

Daedalus's Guides to the Web: Net and Web Resources and Information A great page with links to many lists of Net resources.
http://www.georgetown.edu/labyrinth/general/general.html

Look Smart Not really a search engine, but an extremely well organized subject index of the Web from the folks at *Reader's Digest.* Start with a general subject and then burrow down to the information you're looking for.
http://mulwala.looksmart.com:8080/

Meta-Index of WWW Resources, Library of Congress
A bird's-eye view of resources available on the Web.
http://lcweb.loc.gov/global/explore.html

Meta-Index of WWW and Internet Resources (NCSA)
A general index of the Net.
http://www.ncsa.uiuc.edu/SDG/Software/Mosaic/Meta Index.html

New Riders' Official World Wide Web Yellow Pages
The Web version of a popular reference book. Search by keyword or subject.
http://www.mcp.com/nrp/wwwyp/

Search Engines

Don't let the term *search engine* scare you—all you need to do is type in the subject you're interested in, click on a button, and sit back while these cyber-bloodhounds sniff out the goodies. Each search engine has its own particular strengths and weaknesses, so if at first you don't succeed in finding what you're looking for, try another one. As a matter of fact, try another one even if you think you've succeeded the first time, because there's always more of everything out there on the Net.

All-in-One Search Page A handy site that offers access to

all the major search engines on one Web page. Also offers software and e-mail address searching.
http://www.albany.net/allinone/

Altavista A very powerful search engine based on a full-text index of more than 16 million Web pages.
http://www.altavista.digital.com

Excite Netsearch Also offers reviews of many Web sites.
http://www.excite.com/

Hotbot Very fast and versatile search engine from *Wired* magazine.
http://www.hotbot.com

InfoSeek Home Page Offers both free Web searches and fee-based searches of commercial databases.
http://www.infoseek.com/Home

Lycos Home Page Another very powerful search engine.
http://www.lycos.com/

Magellan Offers minireviews of the sites it finds for you.
http://www.mckinley.com/

SavvySearch Sends your query to fifteen separate search engines, then displays the results in a single list.
http://www.cs.colostate.edu/~dreiling/smartform.html

WebCrawler Searching Good for simple searches; usually very fast.
http://webcrawler.com/

Yahoo! One of the first, and still one of the best Web search engines. Yahoo! also incorporates an excellent browsable index of Web resources.
http://www.yahoo.com

Indexes of Resources for Book Lovers

The indexes listed here include books on-line, bookstores, pointers to literary discussion groups, general literary resources, and links to other more specialized indexes. Many of these indexes and lists, in true hypertext fashion, refer to each other, so any one index will probably lead you eventually to anything found in any other index.

American Studies Web: Literature and Hypertext A list of sites mostly relating to American literature. Includes links to pages devoted to individual authors.
http://www.georgetown.edu/crossroads.asw

Book Lovers: Fine Books and Literature A great resource page for book lovers, frequently updated and worth visiting on a regular basis. The author of the page keeps a sharp eye out for new resources on the Net.
http://www.xs4all.nl/~pwessel/

Book Stacks—Electronic Library Features a wide variety of public domain texts.
http://www.books.com/scripts/lib.exe

BookWeb The American Booksellers Association home page. It offers information on publishers, media, etc., as well as an overview of on-line resources.
http://ambook.org/

BookWire "The First Place to Look for Book Information": Another great site with links to almost everywhere.
http://www.bookwire.com/

BookZone Literary Leaps A great site with more than 1,200 links to literary sites on the Net, organized by subject.
http://www.bookzone.com/leaps/leaps.cfm

Canadian Literature Archive From the University of Manitoba.
http://canlit.st-john.umanitoba.ca/Canlitx/Canlit_homepage.html

The English Server A great site with fascinating content as well as neatly organized links to resources on anything connected to English literature.
http://english-server.hss.cmu.edu/

Frequently Asked Questions (FAQ) About Book Newsgroups Where to find information on a variety of subjects among the many Usenet newsgroups devoted to books and reading.
http://www.cis.ohio-state.edu/hypertext/faq/usenet/books/top.html

Internet Book Information Center Maintains the World Wide Web Virtual Library on Literature, which contains hundreds of links to literary sites on the Net.
http://sunsite.unc.edu/ibic/IBIC-homepage.html

Internet Public Library (IPL) A genuine on-line library, with a reference desk and tons of resources.
http://ipl.sils.umich.edu/

Literature at Yahoo! The folks at Yahoo! do a great job of cataloging literary resources on the Web. They label the new ones, so check here frequently.
http://www.yahoo.com/Arts/Humanities/Literature/

Literature Resources for the High School and College Student An extensive collection of useful links.
http://www.teleport.com/~mgroves/

LitLinks, University of Alberta Links to a wide variety of literary resources.
http://www.ualberta.ca/~amactavi/litlinks.htm

LitWeb A well-organized overview of readers' and writers' resources.
http://www.arcana.com/shannon/litweb.html

On-line Books Page An index developed at Carnegie-Mellon University of over 1,000 on-line books.
http://www.cs.cmu.edu/Web/books.html

OZ Lit An index of Australian literature on-line.
http://www.vicnet.net.au/~ozlit/index.html

Project Gutenberg Master Index The master list of all books converted to e-text by Project Gutenberg. The goal of the project is to make 10,000 texts available on-line by the year 2000.
http://www.promo.net/pg/
Usenet newsgroup: **bit.listserv-gutnberg-1**

Project Runeberg Scandinavian books and culture.
http://www.lysator.liu.se/runeberg/

Rare Books Around the Net Links for bibliophiles.
http://www.abaa-booknet.com/discuss.html

Rec.arts.books FAQ A fourteen-part FAQ file for the primary Usenet newsgroup for book lovers.
http://www.cis.ohio-state.edu:80/hypertext/faq/usenet/books/faq/faq.html

Rec.arts.books Home Page FAQ, bookstore, and book club lists, lots more.
http://www.wco.com/~rteeter/rab.html

UNCAT The catalog of the uncataloged books, newsletters, and more that never made it into *Books in Print.*
http://www.sapphire.com/uncat

VoS English Literature *Voice of the Shuttle* English literature page—covers a broad range of literary genres and periods.
http://humanitas.ucsb.edu/shuttle/english.html

The Word An eclectic list that includes e-zines, on-line books, related resources, and unusual links.
http://www.speakeasy.org/~dbrick/Hot/word.html

The Write Page An excellent collection of resources, arranged by genre.
http://www.writepage.com/

USENET NEWSGROUPS

alt.appalachian.literature
alt.books.beatgeneration
alt.books.technical
bit.listserv-literary
rec.arts.books
sci.classics

Frequently Asked Questions (FAQ) Files

The following list is drawn with permission from Dr. Wolfgang Hink's excellent *Guide to Literature on the Inter-*

net, which includes FAQ and other informational files pertaining to reading and literature. The current version of Dr. Hink's guide is available at **http://spinfo1.spinfo.uni-koeln.de/e-text/Guide.html**.

Many of these FAQs are posted periodically in the relevant newsgroups (noted in the "Newsgroups" line of each item), as well as in the **news.answers** newsgroup.

If there is no archive name listed, wait to see if the FAQ appears in the relevant newsgroup or in the **news.answers** newsgroup, or request the FAQ from the author directly, at the e-mail address noted in each entry.

alt.books.reviews FAQ

Newsgroups: **alt.books.reviews**, **rec.arts.books**, **rec.answers**, **alt.answers**, **news.answers**
From: sbrock@teal.csn.org (Steve Brock)
Archive name: books/reviews-faq

alt.comics.alternative FAQ

Newsgroups: **alt.comics.alternative**
From: kap1@wimpy.cpe.uchicago.edu (Dietrich J. Kappe)

alt.cyberpunk FAQ

Newsgroups: **alt.cyberpunk**, **alt.answers**, **news.answers**
From: erich@hrl8.cs.tamu.edu (Erich Schneider)
Archive name: cyberpunk-faq

alt.fan.douglas-adams FAQ

Newsgroups: **alt.fan.douglas-adams**, **alt.answers**, **news.answers**

From: nhughes@tiamat.umd.umich.edu (Nathan Hughes)
Archive name: douglas-adams-FAQ

alt.fan.dune FAQ
Newsgroups: **alt.fan.dune**, **alt.answers**, **news.answers**
From: cgilmore@phoenix.princeton.edu
Archive name: sf/dune-faq

alt.fan.pern FAQ
Newsgroups: **alt.fan.pern**, **news.answers**, **alt.answers**
From: quirk@unm.edu (Taki Kogoma)
Archive name: pern-intro/part1 [-2]

alt.fan.piers-anthony FAQ
Newsgroups: **alt.fan.piers-anthony**, **alt.answers**, **news.answers**
From: umholme0@cc.UManitoba.CA (Douglas Holmes)
Archive name: books/piers-anthony-faq

alt.fan.pratchett FAQ
Newsgroups: **alt.fan.pratchett**, **news.answers**, **alt.answers**
From: gnat@kauri.vuw.ac.nz (Nathan Torkington)
Archive name: pratchett/faq

alt.fan-pratchett Mini-FAQ
Newsgroups: **alt.fan.pratchett**
From: leo@cp.tn.tudelft.nl (Leo Breebaart)
Archive name: pratchett-mini-faq

alt.folklore.ghost-stories FAQ
Newsgroups: **alt.folklore.ghost-stories**, **alt.paranormal**, **alt.paranet.paranormal**, **alt.answers**, **news.answers**
From: obiwan@Netcom.com (obiwan)
Archive name: folklore/ghost-stories

alt.history.what-if FAQ
Newsgroups: **alt.history.what-if**, **alt.answers**, **news.answers**
From: altworld@panix.com (Robert B. Schmunk)
Archive name: history/what-if

alt.quotations FAQ
Newsgroups: **alt.quotations**, **alt.answers**, **news.answers**
From: dok@fwi.uva.nl
Archive name: quotations/part1

alt.sex.stories FAQ
Newsgroups: **alt.sex.stories**, **alt.sex.stories.d**
From: laff@headop.cs.uiuc.edu (Joshua A. Laff)

alt.usage.english FAQ
Newsgroups: **alt.usage.english**, **alt.answers**, **news.answers**
From: misrael@csi.uottawa.ca (Mark Israel)
Archive name: alt-usage-english-faq

Alternate History Stories
Newsgroups: **rec.arts.sf.written**, **alt.history.what-if**, **rec.answers**, **alt.answers**, **news.answers**

From: altworld@panix.com (Robert B. Schmunk)
Archive name: sf/alt_history/part1 [-8]

Arthurian Booklist
Newsgroups: **rec.arts.books**, **rec.answers**, **news.answers**
From: tittle@Netcom.com (Cindy Tittle Moore)
Archive name: books/arthurian

Isaac Asimov FAQ
Newsgroups: **alt.books.isaac-asimov**, **alt.answers**, **news.answers**
From: John_Jenkins@taligent.com (John H. Jenkins)
Archive name: books/isaac-asimov-faq/part1 [-2]

Basement Full of Books
Newsgroups: **rec.arts.books**, **rec.answers**, **news.answers**
From: mcintyre@cpac.washington.edu (Vonda N. McIntyre)
Archive name: books/basement-full-of-books

Book Catalogues and Book Clubs List (**rec.arts.books**)
Newsgroups: **rec.arts.books**, **rec.answers**, **news.answers**
From: tittle@Netcom.com (Cindy Tittle Moore)
Archive name: books/catalogues

Books by Mail (FAQ)
Newsgroups: **rec.arts.books**, **rec.arts.sf.written**, **rec.answers**, **news.answers**
From: ecl@mtgp003.mt.att.com (Evelyn C. Leeper)
Archive name: books/ship-by-mail

Bookstores in Eastern North American Cities (FAQ)
Newsgroups: **rec.arts.books**, **rec.arts.sf.written**, **rec.answers**, **news.answers**
From: ecl@mtgp003.mt.att.com (Evelyn C. Leeper)
Archive name: books/stores/north-american/eastern

Bookstores in New York City (NYC) List (FAQ)
Newsgroups: **rec.arts.books**, **rec.arts.sf.written**, **ny.general**, **nyc.general**, **nj.general**, **rec.answers**, **news.answers**
From: ecl@mtgp003.mt.att.com (Evelyn C. Leeper)
Archive name: books/stores/north-american/nyc

Bookstores in Northern North American Cities (FAQ)
Newsgroups: **rec.arts.books**, **rec.arts.sf.written**, **rec.answers**, **news.answers**
From: ecl@mtgp003.mt.att.com (Evelyn C. Leeper)
Archive name: books/stores/north-american/northern

Bookstores in San Diego
Newsgroups: **rec.arts.books**, **rec.arts.books.childrens**, **la.forsale**, **relcom.fido.su.books**
From: jamesd@cg57.esNet.com (James Davis)

Bookstores in San Francisco Bay Area (SF) List (FAQ)
Newsgroups: **rec.arts.books**, **rec.arts.sf.written**, **ba.general**, **rec.answers**, **news.answers**
From: ecl@mtgp003.mt.att.com (Evelyn C. Leeper)
Archive name: books/stores/north-american/bay-area

Bookstores in Various Asian Cities List (FAQ)
Newsgroups: **rec.arts.books**, **rec.arts.sf.written**, **rec.answers**, **news.answers**

From: ecl@mtgp003.mt.att.com (Evelyn C. Leeper)
Archive name: books/stores/asian

Bookstores in Various European Cities List (FAQ)
Newsgroups: **rec.arts.books**, **rec.arts.sf.written**, **rec.answers**, **news.answers**
From: ecl@mtgp003.mt.att.com (Evelyn C. Leeper)
Archive name: books/stores/european

Bookstores in Western North American Cities (FAQ)
Newsgroups: **rec.arts.books**, **rec.arts.sf.written**, **rec.answers**, **news.answers**
From: ecl@mtgp003.mt.att.com (Evelyn C. Leeper)
Archive name: books/stores/north-american/western

Classical Studies FAQ
Newsgroups: **sci.classics**, **sci.answers**, **news.answers**
From: jamie@akeake. its.vuw.ac.nz (Jamieson Norrish)
Archive name: classics-faq

Classics FTP, Gopher, WWW, etc., Sites
Newsgroups: **sci.classics**
From: jsruebel@iastate.edu (James S. Ruebel)

Grading Guide (To Preserve and Protect Comics)
Newsgroups: **rec.arts.comics.info**, **rec.arts.comics.misc**
From: paul@erc.msstate.edu (Paul Adams)

Grading Guide (Grading Comics)
Newsgroups: **rec.arts.comics.info**, **rec.arts.comics.marketplace**
From: paul@erc.msstate.edu (Paul Adams)

Internet Mall: Shopping the Information Highway
Newsgroups: **alt.internet.services**, **comp.newprod**, **alt.answers**, **comp.answers**, **news.answers**
From: taylor@netcom.com (Dave Taylor)
Archive name: Internet-services/Internet-mall

Internet Top 100 SF List FAQ
Newsgroups: **rec.arts.books**
From: tcooke@maths.adelaide.edu.au (Tristrom Cooke)

Internet Writer Resource Guide
Newsgroups: **misc.writing**, **rec.arts.prose**, **rec.arts.sf.written**, **misc.answers**, **rec.answers**, **news.answers**
From: t.lawrence@auntie.bbcnc.org.uk (Trevor Lawrence)
Archive name: writing/resources

Journalism Resources on the Internet
Newsgroups: **alt.journalism**, **alt.politics.media**, **alt.news-media**, **alt.answers**, **news.answers**
From: verbwork@access.digex.net (John S. Makulowich)
Archive name: journalism-Net-resources

James Joyce FAQ
Newsgroups: **rec.arts.books**
From: jorn@MCS.COM (Jorn Barger)

Media List
Newsgroups: **alt.journalism**, **alt.internet.services**
From: adamg@world.std.com (Adam M. Gaffin)

misc.books.technical FAQ

Newsgroups: **misc.books.technical**, **misc.answers**, **news.answers**

From: rathinam@worf.infonet.net (Sethu R. Rathinam)

Archive name: books/technical

misc.writing FAQ

Newsgroups: **misc.writing**, **news.answers**, **misc.answers**

From: lsefton@apple.com

Archive name: writing/FAQ

misc.writing FAQ: Recommended Reading

Newsgroups: **misc.writing**, **misc.answers**, **news.answers**

From: lsefton@apple.com

Archive name: writing/bibliography

Murder Mysteries Set in Ancient Rome (Booklist)

Newsgroups: **rec.arts.mystery**, **sci.classics**, **alt.books.reviews**

From: heli@netcom.com (Rick Heli)

Nautical Fiction List [2 parts]

Newsgroups: **rec.arts.books**, **rec.boats**

From: jkohnen@efn.org (John Kohnen)

On-line Book Publisher List

Newsgroups: **rec.arts.books**, **rec.arts.books.marketplace**, **rec.arts.books.childrens**, **rec.arts.mystery**

From: brock@ucsub.Colorado.edu (Steve Brock)

On-line Books FAQ
Newsgroups: **alt.etext**, **rec.arts.books**, **alt.internet.services**, **sci.classics**
From: dell@wiretap.spies.com (Thomas Dell)

On-line Bookstores List
Newsgroups: **rec.arts.books**, **rec.arts.books.marketplace**, **rec.arts.books.childrens**, **rec.arts.mystery**
From: brock@ucsub.Colorado.edu (Steve Brock)

Terry Pratchett Bibliography
Newsgroups: **alt.fan.pratchett**, **news.answers**, **alt.answers**
From: gnat@kauri.vuw.ac.nz (Nathan Torkington)
Archive name: pratchett/bibliography

Project Gutenberg List of Etext (Part I)
Project Gutenberg List of Etext (Part II)
Newsgroups: **alt.etext**
From: dircompg@sunee.uwaterloo.ca (Project Gutenberg)

Thomas Pynchon FAQ
Newsgroups: **rec.arts.books**
From: jorn@mcs.com (Jorn Barger)

rec.arts.books bookstores list: Cambridge/Boston
Newsgroups: **rec.arts.books**
From: nichael@bbn.com (Nichael Cramer)

rec.arts.books FAQ
Newsgroups: **rec.arts.books**, **rec.answers**, **news.answers**

From: ecl@mtgp003.mt.att.com (Evelyn C. Leeper)
Archive name: books/faq

rec.arts.comics FAQ
Newsgroups: **rec.arts.comics.info**, **rec.arts.comics.misc**, **rec.answers**, **news.answers**
From: tyg@hq.ileaf.com (Tom Galloway)
Archive name: comics/faq/part1 [-7]

rec.arts.sf groups, an introduction
Newsgroups: **rec.arts.sf.announce**, **rec.arts.sf.misc**, **rec.answers**, **news.answers**
From: felan@netcom.com (Leanne Phillips)
Archive name: sf/groups-intro

rec.arts.sf.reviews FAQ
Newsgroups: **rec.arts.sf.reviews**, **rec.answers**, **news.answers**
From: djdaneh@pbhyc.pacbell.com
Archive name: sf/reviews-faq

rec.arts.sf.written FAQ
Newsgroups: **rec.arts.sf.written**, **rec.arts.sf.misc**, **news.answers**, **rec.answers**
From: burchard@access.digex.net (Laura Burchard)
Archive name: sf/written-intro

rec.arts.sf.written.robert-jordan FAQ
Newsgroups: **rec.arts.sf.written.robert-jordan**, **rec.arts.sf.written**, **rec.answers**, **news.answers**
From: joeshaw@info1.cc.vt.edu (Joe "Uno" Shaw)
Archive name: sf/robert-jordan-faq

rec.arts.theatre FAQ
Newsgroups: **rec.arts.theatre.musicals**,

rec.arts.theatre.misc, **rec.arts.theatre.plays**, **rec.answers**, **news.answers**
From: aku@leland.Stanford.edu (Andrew Chia-Tso Ku)
Archive name: theatre/part1 [-3]

Anne Rice FAQ
Newsgroups: **alt.books.anne-rice**, **alt.answers**, **news.answers**
From: lat13@columbia.edu (Laura Ann)

Robin Hood Booklist
Newsgroups: **rec.arts.books**, **rec.answers**, **news.answers**
From: tittle@netcom.com (Cindy Tittle Moore)
Archive name: books/robin-hood

SF-references-in-music list
Newsgroups: **rec.music.misc**, **rec.arts.sf.misc**, **rec.answers**, **news.answers**
From: rsk@aspen.circ.upenn.edu (Rich Kulawiec)
Archive name: music/sci-fi-refs

Shakespeare in Star Trek
Newsgroups: **rec.arts.startrek.misc**
From: petersm@csos.orst.edu (Marguerite Petersen)

Sherlock Holmes Booklist (FAQ)
Newsgroups: **rec.arts.books**, **alt.fan.holmes**, **alt.answers**, **rec.answers**, **news.answers**
From: ecl@mtgp003.mt.att.com (Evelyn C. Leeper)
Archive name: books/holmes/list

Sherlock Holmes Illustrated
Newsgroups: **rec.arts.books**, **alt.fan.holmes**, **rec.answers**, **alt.answers**, **news.answers**

From: mlbm@lanl.gov (Mark Martinez)
Archive name: books/holmes/illustrated

Star Trek: Bibliography of ST Articles/Books
Newsgroups: **rec.arts.startrek.misc**
From: wright@facl.lan.mcgill.ca (J. Wright)

Star Trek Book Guide
Newsgroups: **rec.arts.startrek.fandom**, **rec.answers**, **news.answers**
From: kevina@clark.Net (Kevin Atkinson)
Author: Arnold E. van Beverhoudt, Jr.
71777.2365@compuserve.com
Archive name: star-trek/CS-guide/books/part1 [-2]

Superman FAQ
Newsgroups: **rec.arts.comics.info**, **rec.arts.comics.misc**, **alt.comics.superman**
From: davidc@leland.Stanford.edu (David Thomas Chappell)
Archive name: superman-faq

Titles of Comics Collections
Newsgroups: **rec.arts.comics.strips**, **rec.answers**, **news.answers**
From: dkrause@hydra.acs.uci.edu (Doug Krause)
Archive name: comics/collections

J.R.R. Tolkien: Frequently Asked Questions
Newsgroups: **rec.arts.books.tolkien**, **alt.fan.tolkien**, **rec.answers**, **alt.answers**, **news.answers**

From: loos@frodo.mgh.harvard.edu (William D.B. Loos)
Archive name: tolkien/faq/part1[-2]

J.R.R. Tolkien: Less Frequently Asked Questions
Newsgroups: **rec.arts.books.tolkien**, **alt.fan.tolkien**, **rec.answers**, **alt.answers**, **news.answers**
From: loos@frodo.mgh.harvard.edu (William D.B. Loos)
Archive name: tolkien/lessfaq/part1

Zines on the Internet
Newsgroups: **alt.zines**, **alt.etext**, **misc.writing**, **rec.mag**, **alt.Internet.services**, **alt.answers**, **misc.answers**, **rec.answers**, **news.answers**
From: johnl@netcom.com (John Labovitz)
Archive name: writing/zines/part1 [-5]

ON-LINE SERVICES

America Online

The Book Report (keyword: book report)
Reviews, recommendations, a newsletter, kids' area, live author events, a chat room, author-specific fan discussion groups, and more.

The Book Nook (keyword: book nook)
Bestseller list, chat room, message boards.

Rogueprint (keyword: rogueprint)
Author interviews and "Hidden Gems," great works of fiction that are often overlooked.

Book Central (keyword: bc)
Books and author information, live events, and 137 member-run reading groups.

The WELL: The Books Conference
A forum to discuss all facets of books and reading.

BOOKS AND AUTHORS

Authors

GENERAL INDEXES OF AUTHORS

Book Stacks—Author's Pen Excellent site with links to more than 800 Web pages devoted to authors.
http://www.books.com/scripts/authors.exe

Books On-line: Authors A searchable index of authors.
http://www.cs.cmu.edu/Web/bookauthors.html

Bookwire Author Indexes A very good index of directories.
http://www.bookwire.com/index/author-indexes.html

British and Irish Authors on the Web Chronologically indexed.
http://lang.nagoya-u.ac.jp/~matsuoka/UK-authors.html

Great Writers An extensive list of writers' home pages.
http://www.xs4all.nl/~pwessel/writers.html

Literary Kicks A page devoted to Beat authors.
http://www.charm.net/~brooklyn/LitKicks.html

Literary Menagerie Links to authors' home pages.
http://sunset.backbone.olemiss.edu/~egcash/

Literascape Links to "Literary" authors' pages.
http://www.literascape.com/Friends/Authors/

BohemianLink Another lively Beat site.
http://www.levity.com/corduroy/index.htm

Yahoo! Net Events: Authors See if your favorite author is on-line tonight.
http://events.yahoo.com/Arts_and_Entertainment/Books_and_Literature/Authors/

USENET NEWSGROUP

alt.books.beatgeneration

RESOURCES DEVOTED TO SPECIFIC AUTHORS

Most of the Web pages, Usenet newsgroups, and mailing lists given here are created by fans of the particular writer. A few authors have taken an active interest in their Web sites, and Douglas Adams is known to have posted to the **alt.fan.douglas-adams** newsgroup.

Almost all of the Web pages listed here offer a short biography, a bibliography, and links to other Net resources devoted to the author of his or her genre or era.

This list is merely a sampling of all the Web pages on the Net devoted to authors, so your favorite author may not appear here. But that doesn't mean that he or she doesn't have a Web page, mailing list, or newsgroup on the Net. Just check at the Author's Pen Web site mentioned above (**http://www.books.com/scripts/authors.exe**) or fire up one of the search engines listed on page 127 to track down the author's name. And if you find that there is, indeed, not yet a Web page, mailing list, or newsgroup for your favorite author, that simply means that it's up to you to create one.

The Douglas Adams Worship Page
http://www.umd.umich.edu/~nhughes/dna/
Usenet newsgroup: **alt.fan.douglas-adams**

Louisa May Alcott
http://www.coppersky.com/louisa/

Dante Alighieri Digital Dante courtesy of Columbia University
http://www.ilt.columbia.edu/projects/dante/index.html

Martin Amis
http://www.albion.edu/fac/engl/diedrick/amispge.htm
Usenet newsgroup: **alt.fan.martin-amis**

Maya Angelou
http://www.cwrl.utexas.edu/~mmaynard/Maya/maya 5.html

Isaac Asimov
http://www.clark.net/pub/edseiler/WWW/ asimov_home_page.html
Usenet newsgroup: **alt.books.isaac-asimov**

Margaret Atwood
http://www.web.net/owtoad/

Jane Austen Information Page and a fascinating presentation of *Pride and Prejudice* in hypertext.
http://uts.cc.utexas.edu/~churchh/janeinfo.html
Mailing list: **AUSTEN-L**
Mail to: **listserv@vm1.mcgill.ca**

Paul Auster
http://curry.edschool.virginia.edu/~jef2e/auster/ auster.html

J.G. Ballard
http://www.geocities.com/Area51/Corridor/4085/ballard.html

Julian Barnes
http://alexia.lis.uiuc.edu/~roberts/barnes/home.htm

Aphra Behn
http://ourworld.compuserve.com/homepages/r_nestvold/

Saul Bellow
http://www.almaz.com/nobel/literature/1976a.html

Ambrose Bierce
http://nti.uji.es/CPE/ed/0.0/bierce/

The William Blake Page—Devoted to the works of the great English Romantic poet, painter, engraver, and printer. Includes writings, poetry, and art, plus links to other Blake resources on-line.
http://www.aa.net/~urizen/blake.html

André Breton
http://www.lm.com/~kalin/breton.html

The Brontës (Emily, Charlotte, and Anne)
Mailing list: **Bronte**
Mail to: **majordomo@world.std.com**

Charlotte Brontë
http://www.stg.brown.edu/projects/hypertext/landow/victorian/cbronte/bronteov.html

Emily Brontë
http://sunsite.unc.edu/cheryb/women/Emily-Bronte.html

Charles Bukowski
http://realbeer.com/buk/

William S. Burroughs Page
http://www.inch.com/~ari/words1.html

Italo Calvino
http://userwww.service.emory.edu/~mpajare/cal.html

Albert Camus
http://www.inch.com/~ari/words1.html

Truman Capote
http://www.levity.com/corduroy/capote.htm

Lewis Carroll
http://www.lewiscarroll.org/carroll.html

Raymond Carver
http://world.std.com/~ptc/

Willa Cather
http://icg.fas.harvard.edu/~cather/

Miguel de Cervantes
Mailing list: **CERVNTES**
Mail to: **listserv@listserv.acns.nwu.edu**

Geoffrey Chaucer
http://www.vmi.edu/~english/chaucer.html
Mailing list: **Chaucer**
Mail to: **listserv@uicvm.uic.edu**

Anton Chekhov
http://www.winnipeg.freenet.mb.ca/~vbu053/Anton_Chekhov.html

Arthur C. Clarke
http://www.lsi.usp.br/~rbianchi/clarke/
Usenet newsgroup: **alt.books.arthur-clarke**

S. T. Coleridge Home Page Major works, biographical information, and assorted materials.
http://www.lib.virginia.edu/etext/stc/Coleridge/stc.html

Wilkie Collins Appreciation Page Inventor of the modern detective story.
http://www.ozemail.com.au/~drgrigg/wilkie.html

Michael Crichton
http://http.tamu.edu:8000/~cmc0112/crichton.html

e. e. cummings
http://members.tripod.com/~Dwipf/cummings.html

Don DeLillo
http://haas.berkeley.edu/~gardner/delillo.html

Charles Dickens Dickens Home Page Scholarly papers, conferences, and links to other on-line Dickens resources.
http://lang.nagoya-v.ac.up./~matsvoka/Dickens.html
Mailing list: **DICKNS-L**
Mail to: **listserv@ucsbvm.ucsb.edu**

Emily Dickinson Scholarly essays, links to works on-line, and a mailing list.
http://www.planet.net/pkrisxle/emily/dickinson.html

Arthur Conan Doyle
http://www.cs.cmu.edu/afs/andrew.cmu.edu/usr18/mset/www/holmes.html
Usenet newsgroup: **alt.fan.holmes**
Mailing list: **HOUNDS-L (Sherlock Holmes Literature)**
Mail to: **listserv@kentvm.kent.edu**

Daphne Du Maurier
http://www.wdi.co.uk/westwind/cornwall/daphne/maurier.html

Marguerite Duras
http://www.uta.fi/~trkisa/duras/duras.html

Umberto Eco
http://www4.ncsu.edu/eos/users/m/mcmesser/www/eco.html/

T. S. Eliot
http://www.deathclock.com/morpheus/thunder/

William Faulkner
http://cypress.mcsr.olemiss.edu/~egjbp/faulkner/faulkner.html

F. Scott Fitzgerald
http://www.csd.scarolina.edu/fitzgerald/index.html

Lawrence Ferlinghetti
http://www.charm.net/~brooklyn/People/LawrenceFerlinghetti.html

Ian Fleming
http://www.mcs.net/~klast/www/fleming.html

Benjamin Franklin: Glimpses of the Man
http://sln.fi.edu/franklin/rotten.html

Elizabeth Gaskell
http://lang.nagoya-u.ac.jp/~matsuoka/Gaskell.html

André Gide
http://www.lm.com/~kalin/gide.html

Allen Ginsberg
http://www.ginzy.com/

Nikki Giovanni
http://athena.english.vt.edu/Giovanni/Nikki_Giovanni.html

Sue Grafton
http://www.suegrafton.com/

Robert Graves
http://faculty.ed.umuc.edu/~rschumak/bio_rg.htm

John Grisham
http://www.privat.katedral.se/~nv96gabr/grisham.htm

Knut Hamsun
http://home.sn.no/~kromanna/hamsun.html

Thomas Hardy
http://www.prestigeweb.com/hardy/

Nathaniel Hawthorne
http://www.tiac.net/users/eldred/nh/hawthorne.html

Seamus Heaney
http://sunsite.unc.edu/dykki/poetry/heaney/heaney-cov.html

Robert Heinlein
http://fly.hiwaay.net/~hester/heinlein.html
Usenet newsgroup: **alt.fan.heinlein**

Joseph Heller
http://www.levity.com/corduroy/heller.htm

Mark Helprin
http://www.rigroup.com/~candi/helprin/

Ernest Hemingway
http://www.ee.mcgill.ca/~nverever/hem/cover.html

Hermann Hesse
http://www.mcl.ucsb.edu/hesse/
Mailing list: **HESSE-L**
Mail to: **listserv@cmsa.berkeley.edu**

A. E. Housman
http://library.utoronto.ca/www/utel/rp/authors/housman.html

Zora Neale Hurston
http://pages.prodigy.com/zora/index.htm

Victor Hugo
http://www.ot.com/lesmis/hugo.html

John Irving
http://members.aol.com/forestben/irving.htm

Jane Jacobs
http://palladio.arch.virginia.edu/~plan303/

Henry James
http://www.newpaltz.edu/~hathaway/

Samuel Johnson
http://www.english.upenn.edu/~jlynch/Johnson/

James Joyce—Work in Progress: James Joyce in Cyberspace
http://www.2street.com/joyce/
Mailing list: **FWAKE-L** (*Finnegan's Wake* Discussion List)
Mail to: **listserv@irlearn.bitnet**

Franz Kafka—Texts, biographical material, and links to other resources.
http://www.family.knick.net/thecastle/

Nikos Kazantzakis
http://www.interkriti.org/culture/kazantzakis/kazantz2.htm

John Keats
http://www.columbia.edu/acis/bartleby/keats/

John Kerouac
http://www.charm.net/~brooklyn/People/Jack Kerouac.html

Stephen King
http://www.geocities.com/area51/zone/1563/
Usenet newsgroup: **alt.books.stephen-king**

Rudyard Kipling
http://www.accinet.net/~fjzwick/kipling/

Milan Kundera
http://www.georgetown.edu/irvinemj/english016/kundera/kundera.html

Anne Lamott
http://www.typo.com/lamott/lamott.html

Ring Lardner
http://ourworld.compuserve.com/homepages/Topping/

D. H. Lawrence
http://home.clara.net/rananim/lawrence

Edward Lear
http://www2.pair.com/mgraz/Lear/index.html

Doris Lessing
http://tile.net/lessing/index.html

Primo Levi Page Biography, bibliography, and an interview with the author.
http://inch.com/~ari/levi1.html

C. S. Lewis
http://ernie.bgsu.edu/~edwards/lewis.html
Usenet newsgroup: **alt.books.cs-lewis**

Wyndham Lewis
http://130.54.80.49/Lewis/Lewis.html

Jack London
http://www.parks.sonoma.net/JLStory.html
Mailing list: **JACK-LONDON**
Mail to: **jack-london-request@sonoma.edu**

H.P. Lovecraft
http://www.primenet.com/~dloucks/hpl/

Joyce Maynard
http://www.joycemaynard.com/

Cormac McCarthy
http://www.cormacmccarthy.com/

John D. MacDonald
http://pages.prodigy.net/mwarble/slipf18/mcgee/

Carson McCullers
http://www.uwf.edu/~English/mccullers/main.htm

Herman Melville
http://www.melville.org/melville.htm

James Michener
http://www.jamesmichener.com/

A. A. Milne
http://www.public.iastate.edu/~jmilne/pooh/milne.html

John Milton John Milton Page—Home page of the MILTON-L mailing list. Offers links to mailing list archives and other Milton resources on-line.
http://www.urich.edu/~creamer/milton.html
Mailing list: **MILTON-L** (John Milton List)
Mail to: **milton-request@urvax.bitnet**

Yukio Mishima
http://www.ibm.park.org/Japan/hometown/yamanakako/mishima/index-e.html

Margaret Mitchell
http://www.student.mckenna.edu/student/ns/tpham/gwtw.html

Lucy Maud Montgomery
http://www.upei.ca/~lmmi/core.html

William Morris
http://www.ccny.cuny.edu/wmorris/morris.html

Toni Morrison
http://www.luminarium.org/contemporary/tonimorrison/toni.htm

H.H. Munro (Saki)
http://www.crl.com/~subir/saki/

Haruki Murakami
http://www.geocities.com/paris/3954/haruki1.htm

Vladimir Nabokov
http://www.libraries.psu.edu/iasweb/nabokov/nsintro.htm
Mailing list: **NABOKV-L**
Mail to: **listserv@ucsbvm.ucsb.edu**

Ogden Nash
http://web.aimnet.com/~veeceet/kids/nash.html

Phyllis Naylor
http://www.childrensbookguild.org/phyllisnaylor.htm

Pablo Neruda
http://www.uic.edu/~pnavia/neruda.html

Anaïs Nin
http://www.dol.com/nin/

Joyce Carol Oates
Celestial Timepiece: A Joyce Carol Oates Home Page
http://storm.usfca.edu/~southerr/jco.html

Patrick O'Brian
http://www.wwnorton.com/pob/pobhome.htm

Flann O'Brien (aka Myles na gCopaleen)
http://indigo.ie/~ocaooai/flindex.html

Ben Okri
http://humanitas.ucsb.edu/users/rbennett/okri/okrigate.html

George Orwell
http://www.levity.com/corduroy/orwell.htm

Dorothy Parker
http://www.levity.com/corduroy/parker.htm

Boris Pasternak
http://nobelprizes.com/nobel/literature/1958a.html

Walker Percy
http://sunsite.unc.edu/wpercy/

Terry Pratchett
http://connexus.apana.org.au/~orin/pterry.html
Usenet newsgroup: **alt.books.pratchett**

Marcel Proust
http://www.proust.com/index.html
Proust Said That—An e-zine from the Marcel Proust Support Group.
http://www.well.com/www/vision/proust

Aleksandr Pushkin
http://falcon.jmu.edu/~gouldsl/Pushkin/

Thomas Pynchon
http://www.pomona.edu/pynchon/index.html
Mailing list: **PYNCHON** (Thomas Pynchon Discussion)
Mail to: **userdog1@sfu.bitnet**
Mailing list: **PYNCHON-L**
Mail to: Contact the list moderator, John K. Gilbert, at **gilbert@sfu.ca.**

Ayn Rand
http://www.vix.com/pub/objectivism/

Mary Renault
http://www.wwu.edu/~stephan/Renault/renault.html

Anne Rice
http://www.annerice.com/
Anne Rice's newsletter, Commotion Strange,
http://earthsystems.org/~shay/commotion.html
Usenet newsgroup: **alt.books.anne-rice**
Mailing list: **ARBOOKS** (Discussion of books by Anne Rice)
Mail to: **LISTSERV@PSUVM.PSU.EDU**

Alain Robbe-Grillet Bibliography and other information on the French novelist.
http://www.halfaya.org/robbegrillet/

Tom Robbins The Tom Robbins Homepage
http://www.rain.org/~da5e/tom_robbins.html
Usenet newsgroup: **alt.fan.tom-robbins**
Mailing list: **MAGIC-L**
Mail to: **listserv@AMERICAN.Edu**

Philip Roth
http://omni.cc.purdue.edu/~royald/roth.htm

Dante Gabriel Rossetti
http://jefferson.village.virginia.edu/rossetti/rossetti.html

Salman Rushdie
http://www.crl.com/~subir/rushdie.html

Antoine de Saint-Exupéry
http://www.westegg.com/exupery/

J. D. Salinger
http://killdevilhill.com/salingerchat/wwwboard.html

Anne Sexton
http://www.inch.com/~aoi/as1.html

William Shakespeare
The Shakespeare Web
The complete works in hypertext.
http://www.shakespeare.com/

Shakespeare Homepage The complete works, in hypertext.
http://the-tech.mit.edu/Shakespeare/works.html
Usenet newsgroup: **humanities.lit.authors.shakespeare**
Mailing list: **SHAKSPER** (Shakespeare Electronic Conference)
Mail to: **listserv@utoronto.bitnet**

Upton Sinclair
http://venus.twu.edu/~S_2stone/upton.html

Aleksandr Isaevich Solzhenitsyn
http://www.almaz.com/nobel/Solzhenitsyn.html

Terry Southern
http://www.charm.net/~brooklyn/People/TerrySouthern.html

Edmund Spenser
http://darkwing.uoregon.edu/~rbear/

John Steinbeck John Steinbeck Research Center, San José State University
http://www.sjsu.edu/depts/steinbec/srchome.html

Robert Louis Stevenson
http://www.rit.edu/~exb1874/mine/stevenson/stevenson-ind.html

Harriet Beecher Stowe
http://www.cs.cmu.edu/People/mmbt/women/StoweHB.html

Jonathan Swift
http://www.incompetech.com/Helpdesk/Authors/swift/

Amy Tan
http://www.luminarium.org/comtemporary/amytan/

The Tennyson Page Features a timeline of Tennyson's life as well as his poems.
http://charon.sfsu.edu/TENNYSON/tennyson.html

William Makepeace Thackeray
http://ernie.lang.nagoya-u.ac.jp/~matsuoka/Thackeray.html

Dylan Thomas
http://pcug.org.au/~wwhatman/dylan_thomas.html

Hunter S. Thompson
http://www.scrod.com/hst/

James Thurber
http://home.earthlink.net/~ritter/thurber/index.html

J.R.R. Tolkien
http://godzilla.eecs.berkeley.edu/rolozo/index.html
Usenet newsgroups: **alt.fan.tolkien, rec.arts.books.tolkien**
Mailing list: **TOLKIEN**
Mail to: **listserv@jhuvm.hcf.jhu.edu**

Leo Tolstoy
ftp://users.aol.com/Tolstoy28/tolstoy.htm

John Kennedy Toole
http://www.levity.com/corduroy/toole.htm

Anthony Trollope
http://www.stg.brown.edu/projects/hypertext/landow/victorian/trollope/trollopeov.html
Mailing list: **TROLLOPE**
Mail to: **majordomo@world.std.com**

Mark Twain
http://web.syr.edu/~fjzwick/twainwww.html
Mailing list: **TWAIN-L**
Mail to: **listserv@vm1.yorku.ca**

John Updike
http://www.users.fast.net/~joyerkes/

Andrew Vachss
http://www.vachss.com/

Jules Verne
http://www.math.technion.ac.il/~rl/JulesVerne/

Voltaire

http://www.mala.bc.ca/~mcneil/volt.htm

Kurt Vonnegut

http://www.cas.usf.edu/english/boon/vonnegut/kv.html

Usenet newsgroup: **alt.books.kurt-vonnegut**

Alice Walker

http://www.luminarium.org/contemporary/alicew/

Evelyn Waugh

http://e2.empirenet.com/~jahvah/waugh/

Eudora Welty

http://www.geocities.com/BourbonStreet/3156/welty.html

Walt Whitman Walt Whitman Home Page. From the U.S. Library of Congress.

http://lcweb2.loc.gov/ammem/wwhome.html

Oscar Wilde

http://www.jonno.com/oscariana/1.html

Laura Ingalls Wilder

http://webpages.marshall.edu/~irby1/laura.htmlx

Thornton Wilder

http://www.sky.net/~emily/thornton.html

William Carlos Williams

http://www.charm.net/~brooklyn/People/WilliamCarlosWilliams. html

P. G. Wodehouse

http://mech.math.msu.su/~gmk/pgw.htm

Usenet newsgroup: **alt.fan.wodehouse**

Thomas Wolfe
http://www.cms.uncwil.edu/~connelly/wolfe.html

Virginia Woolf
http://www.aianet.or.jp/~orlando/VWW/

Richard Wright
http://www.itvs.org/programs/RW/

Roger Zelazny
http://www.enol.com/~ferenczy/rogerz.html

Children's Books and Reading Resources

Amid the media hoopla over the danger of children accessing adult materials on the Internet, very little attention has been given to wonderful sites designed specifically for (and often by) children. Many children's pages have won "Best of the Net" awards and are worth a visit, even if you don't happen to have a child in your home. Good places to start are:

Children's Literature and Language Resources A comprehensive overview for teachers and parents
http://falcon.jmu.edu/~ramseyil/childlit.htm

The Children's Literature Web Guide Provides an excellent overview of the field.
http://www.ucalgary.ca/~dkbrown/index.html

Other notable sites include:

Alice's Adventures in Wonderland By Lewis Carroll, with original illustrations.
http://www.literature.org/works/lewis-carroll/alice-in-wonderland/

Anne of Avonlea
http://www.cs.cmu.edu/People/rgs/avon-table.html

Anne of the Island
http://www.cs.cmu.edu/Web/People/rgs/ann-table.html

Banph Illustrated story of an ant knight.
http://www.banph.com/

The Book Pile Features reviews, stories, and book lists for children ages seven to fourteen. Started by Emily Stephens (when she was thirteen years old), who also directed the construction of the Web site.
http://www.ncf.carleton.ca/~ak001

The Frog King Hypertext "The Frog King," an illustrated Grimm Brothers tale.
http://www.fln.vcu.edu/Grimm/frog.html

Garrett's Stories By Garrett Landon (age nine) and his sister Lucy (age seven).
http://www.scruznet.com/~rlandon/garrett/

Goosebumps Official site of the popular book series.
http://place.scholastic.com/goosebumps/index.htm

Index of Kids' Stories on the WWW Rated and frequently updated.
http://home.earthlink.net/~merlin200/soap/kids.htm

Kidzpage Poetry for children.
http://web.aimnet.com/~veeceet/kids/kidzpage.html

KidPub WWW Publishing KidPub is a place for children to publish stories on the World Wide Web and to read stories published by other children.
http://www.kidpub.org/kidpub/

thekids.com Illustrated stories and poetry from around the world. Includes a chat area for children.
http://www.thekids.com/kids/

Kidstuff A place for kids to write their own stories about space.
http://www.worldchat.com/public/kidstuff/a.htm

A Little Princess The classic story by Frances Hodgson Burnett.
http://www.inform.umd.edu:8080/EdRes/Topic/WomensStudies/ReadingRoom/Fiction/LittlePrincess

Magic School Bus Fun Place Official site of the popular science series.
http://place.scholastic.com/magicschoolbus/index.htm

Mark Twain's Struwwelpeter This hypertext edition of Hoffmann's classic children's story incorporates the original illustrations. Translations by Mark Twain and others.
http://www./Struwwelpeter.com

Poetry for Kids by Kenn Nesbitt
http://www.nesbitt.com/poetry/

Positively Poetry A home page created by a twelve-year-old interested in writing and reading poetry. Designed for children ages five to fifteen.
http://advicom.net/~e-media/kv/poetry1.html

Realist Wonder Society Home Page A fascinating page featuring stories and poems for and by children.
http://www.wondersociety.com/

Rumpelstiltskin The Grimm Brothers story, in German and English. Original illustrations included.
http://www.fln.vcu.edu/Grimm/rumpeng.html

Tales of Tristan Illustrated adventures of a Cairn terrier.
http://www.teleport.com/~jadams/

Tales of Wonder A variety of children's tales from around the world.
http://itpubs.ucdavis.edu/richard/tales/

Topher's Winnie the Pooh Character Guide
http://www.geocities.com/Enchanted Forest/3278/pooh-guide.html

USENET NEWSGROUPS

alt.arts.storytelling
rec.arts.books
rec.arts.books.childrens

Cultural Studies and Multicultural Literature

CWIS Listings Provides connections to academic Gopher sites devoted to African-American, Asian-American, Native American, Latino, and Chicano resources.
http://www.georgetown.edu/tamlit/cwis/cwis.html

Other notable sites include:

African-American Literature A good overview of on-line resources.
http://www.usc.edu/Library/Ref/Ethnic/black_lit_main.html

Asian and Asian-American Poets
http://www.rothpoem.com/asiapoet.html

Black Facts Online Well-done site devoted to Black history.
http://www.blackfacts.com/

Black New York Magazine Literature, poetry, and news.
http://www.bnym.com/index.htm

A Deeper Shade of Black African-American history and literature.
http://www.ai.mit.edu/~isbell/HFh/black/bhcal-toc.html

Hispanic OnLine Web site of *Hispanic* magazine, a monthly publication for and about Hispanics.
http://www.hisp.com

Index of Native American Authors Online
http://hanksville.phast.umass.edu/poems/poets/index0.html

Interracial Voice A news journal serving the mixed-race/interracial community.
http://www.webcom.com/~intvoice/

Latino Link Stories, columns, and photographs by Latino journalists from the United States and Puerto Rico.
http://www.latinolink.com/

Mosaic, the Black Literary Showcase Previews the latest in Black and Hispanic literature.
http://www.mosaicbooks.com/

Native Web
http://www.nativeweb.com/

ONE An African-American journal of art, music, and politics.
http://www.clark.net/pub/conquest/one/home.html

Standards International journal of multicultural studies.
http://stripe.colorado.edu/~standard/

The White Man's Burden and Its Critics A critique of colonialism.
http://www.accinet.net/~fjzwick/kipling/

Writing Black USA Covers American black history studies and literature; includes links to source materials.
http://www.keele.ac.uk/depts/as/Literature/amlit.black.html

Gay, Lesbian, and Bisexual Literature

BLK Homie Pages News and information about the black lesbian and gay community.
http://www.blk.com/blkhome.htm

Harvard Gay and Lesbian Review
http://www.hglc.org/hglc/review.htm

Out Magazine On-line version of the print magazine.
http://www.out.com

Queer Nasty Zine A zine dedicated to "radical thought and intelligent humour."
http://www.tripnet.com/q-nasty/

Humor

Much of the humor found on-line focuses on the Internet itself, computers, or college life. Almost all of it is sophomoric. Some notable exceptions:

Canonical Collection of Tom Swifties
http://www.laughnet.net/archive/misc/tomswift.htm

Cat Bathing as a Martial Art It isn't easy. "Cats have no handles. Add the fact that he now has soapy fur, and the problem is radically compounded."
http://gas.physics.usu.edu/~steev/kitty_gallery/catbath.html

How to Tell the Birds From the Flowers Complete text and pictures of the Robert Woods book written in 1907.
http://www.geocities.com/Vienna/2406/cov.html

Monty Python Online How to tell if your parrot is defunct, among other classics.
http://www.pythonline.com/

News of the Weird Archive Stranger-than-fiction news stories.
http://www.nine.org/notw/archive.html

The Onion On-line incarnation of a satirical newspaper from Wisconsin.
http://www.theonion.com/

Private Eye On-line edition of the British satirical magazine.
http://www.intervid.co.uk/intervid/eye/

The Quotable Mark Twain Includes maxims from *Pudd'nhead Wilson.*
http://marktwain.miningco.com/library/texts/bl_maxims3.htm

Scott's Lardnermania "A page devoted to the memory and appreciation of sportswriter, humorist, and short story writer Ring Lardner."
http://www.tridget.com/lardnermania

Shakespearean Insult Server "Thou pribbling common-kissing apple-john!" Reload the page for a new insult every time.
http://alpha.acast.nova.edu/cgi-bin/bard.pl

Strawberry Pop-Tart Blow-Torches Some genuine scientists set out to test the veracity of a Dave Barry column. Very funny, but don't try this at home, kids.
http://www.sci.tamucc.edu/~pmichaud/toast/

SubSITE—Church of the Subgenius Feel the power of Slack. Very funny. Also very, very strange.
http://www.subgenius.com/

Tina's Humor Archives An interesting collection.
http://www2.cybernex.net/~raytina/fun.html

The Straight Dope Collection of fascinating and hilarious newspaper columns by Cecil Adams.
http://www.straightdope.com/
Usenet newsgroup: **alt.fan.cecil-adams**

USENET NEWSGROUPS

alt.fan.dave-barry
alt.folklore.urban
alt.humor.puns
rec.humor
rec.humor.funny

Mystery Literature

The Case—Mystery Site Links A good general resource page for mystery lovers.
http://www.thecase.com/

ClueLass—A Mystery Newsletter Excellent site for readers and aspiring writers.
http://www.slip.net/~cluelass/

Genre Fiction: Mystery and Suspense A great resource for lovers of detective and crime fiction.
http://www.arcana.com/shannon/mystery.html

History of the Mystery Fascinating narrative timeline of mystery fiction from Cicero to Ed McBain.
http://www.mysterynet.com/history/

Murder on the Internet From Random House—Author interviews, excerpts, and mystery news.
http://www.randomhouse.com/BB/MOTI

The Mysterious Homepage Links to anything a mystery lover would want.
http://www.db.dk/dbaa/jbs/homepage.htm

Mystery Connection Discussion of mysteries, their writers, and their readers.
http://emporium.turnpike.net/~mystery/index.html

The Mystery Zone "The first mystery magazine on the Net." Includes stories, reviews, and links to other on-line resources.
http://www.mindspring.com/~walter/mystzone.html

MysteryNet "The hangout for mystery lovers," who could spend their days wandering through this great site. Includes a discussion area for mystery fans.
http://www.mysterynet.com/

Nero Wolfe Home Page Resources for fans of Rex Stout.
http://www.fish.com/~muffy/pages/books/rex_stout/nero_wolfe.html

RARA AVIS Homepage of a free e-mail mailing list devoted to a hard-boiled detective fiction. Archives, links, and subscription information.
http://www.vex.net/~buff/rara-avis/

The Scrolling Mystery Theater Very well done site featuring mystery novels you can read on-line.
http://www.fiction.com/fiction/intro2.html

Sherlockian Holmepage Home of all things Sherlockian.
http://watserv1.uwaterloo.ca/~credmond/sh.html

Tangled-Web British mystery site with links to authors' home pages.
http://www.thenet.co.uk/~hickafric/tangled-web.html

221 Baker Street Another good Holmes site.
http://www.cs.cmu.edu/afs/andrew.cmu.edu/usr18/mset/www/holmes.html

USENET NEWSGROUPS

alt.fan.holmes
bit.listserv.dorothyl
rec.arts.mystery

ON-LINE SERVICES

America Online: Mystery Forum (keyword: fictional realm)

The WELL: The Mystery Conference
Otherwise known as Noir, where all mystery genres are open for discussion.

Poetry Resources

There is an enormous amount of poetry on-line, not just at the sites listed here (many of which hold dozens of links to other poetry resources) but also in the growing number of e-zines, almost all of which publish verse. If you're interested in seeing your own poems published on-line, be sure to investigate the e-zines listed elsewhere in this index. For tips on putting your poems to paper, see the Writing Resources section.

Academy of American Poets The home page of the Academy, which was founded in 1934 to support American poets at all stages of their careers and to foster the appreciation of contemporary verse. It offers information on membership, awards, and Academy programs.
http://www.he.net/~susannah/academy.htm

Aeneid of Virgil Complete on-line.
http://darkwing.uoregon.edu/~joelja/aeneid.html

Blake Web His complete works, indexed, plus a concordance and a biography.
http://www.unomaha.edu/~wwwengl/blakeweb/

British Poetry 1780–1910: A Hypertext Archive An excellent collection of 19th-century poetry, much of it illustrated and annotated.
http://etext.lib.virginia.edu/britpo.html

Database of African-American Poetry A collection of over 2,500 poems.
http://etext.lib.virginia.edu/aapd.html

Electronic Poetry Center Home Page A collection of poetry resources from the University of Buffalo and the Internet as a whole.
http://wings.buffalo.edu/epc/

T.S. Eliot Page Links to works, commentaries, and even a parody or two.
http://virtual.park.uga.edu/~232/eliot.taken.html

Seamus Heaney Works and a biography of the Nobel Prize winner.
http://sunsite.unc.edu/dykki/poetry/heaney/heaney-cov.html

Keats, John. 1884. Poetical Works From Columbia University's Project Bartleby.
http://www.columbia.edu/acis/bartleby/keats/

Lost Poets of the Great War The works of Rupert Brooke, Wilfred Owen, and other poets killed in World War I.
http://www.cc.emory.edu/ENGLISH/LostPoets/

Oscar Wilde Poems Indexed by both title and first line.
http://www.cc.columbia.edu/acis/bartleby/wilde/

Poems by Emily Dickinson The complete edition in e-text from Project Bartleby.
http://www.columbia.edu/acis/bartleby/dickinson/

Poems Poetry Poets A good collection of links to poetry resources on the Net.
http://www.execpc.com/~jon/

Poetic Express Another collective effort. The home pages of poets included are linked to this page, allowing you to jump directly to more of their poetry. Submissions welcome.
http://www.sacramento-news.com/mary3.htm

Poetry at the English Server A fine collection of poems, from Auden to Wordsworth.
http://english-www.hss.cmu.edu/poetry.html

Poetry on the Web Links to "popular poets" as well as new "independent" poets.
http://www.geocities.com/Paris/1416/

Poetry World Home Page A variety of poetry links from around the world.
http://news.std.com/poetryworld/

The Poetry of Yeats
http://www.maths.tcd.ie/pub/yeats/Index.html

Project Bartleby E-texts of poems and writings by Frost, Keats, Millay, etc.
http://www.columbia.edu/acis/bartleby

Shelley, Percy Bysshe *Complete Poetical Works*, from Project Bartleby at Columbia University.
http://www.columbia.edu/acis/bartleby/shelley/

The Shiki Internet Haiku Salon Examples of haiku, information on haiku contests, and links to haiku and other poetry.
http://mikan.cc.matsuyama-u.ac.jp/~shiki/

Dylan Thomas Poems and links from the Dylan Thomas Society of Australia.
http://pcug.org.au/~wwhatman/dylan_thomas.html

ON-LINE SERVICES

The WELL: The Poetry Conference

Discussions cover the strengths and weaknesses of accomplished poets, favorite poetry book hit lists, references for poesy and poetic terms, fundamentals for reading to an audience, and the political value of poetry in society.

Romance Writing

Considering that "romance literature" or "women's fiction" is one of the hottest-selling genres, it's not surprising that there are a growing number of resources on the Net for lovers of romance novels.

Romance Novels and Women's Fiction Offers a good overview of what's available on the Net.
http://www.writepage.com/romance.htm

Other notable sites include:

Byron Romance Port Includes a searchable database of over 30,000 romance stories.
http://www.geocities.com/Athens/8774/

Romance Communications An on-line magazine, featuring reviews, author interviews, and contests.
http://www.romcom.com/home.htm

Romance Novel Database Information on a range of romance novels.
http://www.sils.umich.edu/~sooty/romance

Romance Reading Ring Linked Web sites devoted to romance novels.
http://www.geocities.com/Athens/8774/ring.htm

Romance novels also seem to inspire quite a few of their readers to write women's fiction themselves, and the Net boasts a number of resources for Romance writers.

Romance Central Includes writers' workshops and forums.
http://home1.gte.net/romcen/index1.htm

Slake For the truly obsessed romance fan. Post your own reviews of books you've read, argue with other readers.
http://www.slake.com/

Your Weekly Kiss Romance fan news, features, interviews, bookstore signing calendar, a chat room, and more.
http://www.mindspring.com/~driordan/kiss/

USENET NEWSGROUP

bit.listserv-rra-1 (Romance Readers Anonymous)

ON-LINE SERVICES

America Online: Romance Realm (keyword: fictional realm)

Scholarly Literary Resources

Nowhere are the academic roots of the Net more visible than in the remarkable range of scholarly resources to be found on-line. From Greek mythology to Victorian literature, the Internet offers both the casual browser and the serious researcher high-quality sources and commentary on nearly any period or type of literature. The first stop in your explorations should be:

Literary Resources on the Net An extraordinary collection of scholarly links arranged by historical period. This page was created by Jack Lynch of the University of

Pennsylvania, who also maintains excellent pages devoted to English grammar and 18th-century literature (reachable through this page). It may take months to work your way through this list, but it will be time well spent.
http://www.english.upenn.edu/~jlynch/Lit/

Other notable sites include:

MYTHOLOGY AND FOLKLORE

American Folk—Folklore and Popular Culture, A fascinating site.
http://www.americanfolk.com/

Joseph Campbell Foundation Web Site Files and information on Joseph Campbell, the Joseph Campbell Foundation, and other resources in mythology, comparative religion, and related fields.
http://www.jcf.org/

Creation Stories and Traditional Wisdom This site collects different versions of creation stories from around the world.
http://www.ozemail.com.au/~reed/global/mythstor.html

Cyberlore Central Devoted to the emerging field of folklore about computers.
http://www.pass.wayne.edu/~twk/cc.html

Encyclopedia Mystica A fascinating on-line encyclopedia covering myths, legends, and folklore

of all cultures. Short entries with links to other sources.
http://www.pantheon.org/myth/

Folklore and Mythology Electronic Texts Translations of tales from Europe.
http://www.pitt.edu/~dash/folktexts.html

The Holy Grail The Big Enchilada of mythology. Links and resources.
http://bigdog.engr.arizona.edu/~dkf/grail.html

Legends and Myths in Cornwall Ghost stories and the inside scoop on pixies from the most haunted spot in Great Britain.
http://www.connexions.co.uk/culture/index.htm

Myth and Legend from Ancient Times to the Space Age Everything from werewolves to UFOs, neatly cataloged.
http://pibweb.it.nwu.edu/~pib/myth.htm

Mythopoeic Society "A non-profit international literary and educational organization for the study, discussion, and enjoyment of fantasy and mythic literature."
http://home.earthlink.net/~emfarrell/mythsoc/mythsoc.html

Mythology Page—Creative Minds Unlimited Monthly discussion of a particular area of world mythology.
http://www.create.org/myth

Myths and Legends An extensive set of links to folklore and mythology resources worldwide, listed by nation and culture.
http://pubpages.unh.edu/~cbsiren/myth.html

Tales of Wonder A fine collection of folk and fairy tales from Russia, Siberia, China, and North America.
http://itpubs.ucdavis.edu/richard/tales/

ANCIENT AND CLASSICAL LITERATURE

Alexander the Great Page
http://www.entergroupltd.com/alex_web/

Ancient Sites Very elaborate page, includes chat area.
http://www.ancientsites.com/

Ancient World Web "The Ultimate Index of All Things Ancient."
http://www.julen.net/aw

Chinese Classics
http://www.cnd.org:8009/Classics/

Christian Classics Ethereal Library Links to many early Christian texts.
http://ccel.wheaton.edu/

Classical Resources
http://www.public.iastate.edu/~flng_info/Classics/resources.html

Classics Guide A guide to classical resources on-line.
http://nervm.nerdc.ufl.edu/~blaland/classics.html

Classics Archive A beautifully designed site offering hundreds of Greek and Latin classics.
http://webatomics.com/Classics/

Latina Folia Christi Classical resources on the Net. In Latin.
http://cctr.umkc.edu/user/cdmitchell/latin/index.html

Perseus Project Classical Greek texts in translation.
http://www.perseus.tufts.edu/

Project Libellus Latin and Greek texts.
http://osman.classics.washington.edu/libellus/libellus.html

MEDIEVAL LITERATURE

Online Medieval and Classical Library Scores of links to text and resources.
http://sunsite.berkeley.edu/OMACL/

WWW Medieval Resources Links to discussion groups, libraries, and other Web sites related to medieval resources.
http://ebbs.english.vt.edu/medieval/medieval.ebbs.html

Other notable sites include:

Arthurian Home Page As in King Arthur.
http://calvin.stemnet.nf.ca/~djohnsto/arthur.html

The Canterbury Tales Project Chaucer's classic, with illustrations.
http://www.shef.ac.uk/uni/projects/ctp/index.html

The Electronic Beowulf Full-color digitized images of the original manuscript.
http://www.uky.edu/ArtsSciences/English/Beowulf/

Illuminated Manuscript—Images from the Bodleian Library at Oxford University.
http://rsl.ox.ac.uk/imacat.html

Images from the Book of Kells
http://www.primate.wisc.edu/people/dubois/kells/

Labyrinth Home Page A well-organized overview of medieval literature on-line.
http://www.georgetown.edu/labyrinth/labyrinth-home.html

Piers Plowman Electronic Archive William Langland's 14th-century allegorical dream vision. Texts of all three versions.
http://jefferson.village.virginia.edu/piers/archive.goals.html

Project Runeberg Scandinavian literature.
http://www.lysator.liu.se/runeberg/

RENAISSANCE LITERATURE

Hypertext Renaissance A page devoted to the concept of hypertext as both a metaphor for, and a valuable tool in the study of, Renaissance literature.
http://www.artsci.wustl.edu/~jntolva/

Luminarium Elaborate site showcasing Medieval, Renaissance, and17th-century literature.
http://www.luminarium.org/

The Renaissance on the Web An overview of Net sites devoted to Renaissance art, literature, and society.
http://www.halcyon.com/howlevin/renaissance.html

Shakespeare Homepage Links to the Bard's works.
http://the-tech.mit.edu/Shakespeare/works.html

Voice of the Shuttle/Renaissance An excellent resource with many links.
http://humanitas.ucsb.edu/shuttle/eng-ren.html

18TH-CENTURY AND ROMANTIC LITERATURE

The Romantic Chronology A year-by-year chronology of the Romantic Age, emphasizing the social events as well as the literature of the period.
http://humanitas.ucsb.edu/projects/pack/rom-chrono/chrono.htm

Romanticism on the Net A scholarly electronic journal devoted entirely to Romantic studies. Includes articles, analyses, and links to other resources.
http://users.ox.ac.uk/~scat0385/

VICTORIAN LITERATURE

See also listings of individual authors, page 146.

Mimi Why "Mimi"? Who knows? The menu lists resources pertaining to American authors through the late 19th century.
http://www.keele.ac.uk/depts/as/Literature/amlit.mimi.html

Victorian Women Writers Project Original texts of literary works by British women writers of the late 19th century.
http://www.indiana.edu/~letrs/vwwp/

Victorian Web Overview Late 19th-century literary resources on the Web.
http://www.stg.brown.edu/projects/hypertext/landow/victorian/victov.html

MODERN LITERATURE

See also listings of individual authors, page 146.

The New Reader Journal with reviews of new fiction.
http://www.literascape.com/Readers/index.html

Pulp Fiction Collection (Library of Congress) Information on the library's collection of popular American fiction magazines.
http://lcweb.loc.gov/spcoll/191.html

Sally Anne Picks up where Mimi (see separate entry) leaves off; a repository of 20th-century American literature.
http://www.keele.ac.uk/depts/as/Literature/amlit.sallyanne.html

USENET NEWSGROUPS

humanities.answers
humanities.lit.authors.shakespeare
humanities.misc

Science Fiction, Fantasy, and Horror

Judging by the remarkable number of Web pages and Usenet newsgroups devoted to science fiction, horror, and fantasy books and authors, these genres hold a particular fascination for the denizens of the Internet. There is an enormous amount of material available on-line, and many of the sites have links to workshops for the aspiring sci-fi, horror, or fantasy writer.

SCIENCE FICTION AND FANTASY RESOURCES

Del Rey Books Sample chapters, author interviews, and reader resources from the flagship SF publisher.
http://www.randomhouse.com/delrey/

Doug's SF Reviews Selections from over 200 short reviews and links to other sci-fi resources.
http://www.phys.tcu.edu/~ingram/books.html

Fantasy BookList An extensive list of fantasy authors and their books, including short reviews.
http://www.mcs.net/~finn/home.html

Feminist Science Fiction A directory of science fiction, fantasy, and utopian fiction on the Net written from a feminist perspective.
http://www.feministsf.org

Internet Top 100 SF/Fantasy List Books rated tops in periodic public voting by Internet users.
http://www.clark.net/pub/iz/Books/Top100/top100.html

The Linköping Science Fiction and Fantasy Archive Links to a wide variety of resources from around the world.
http://sf.www.lysator.liu.se/sf_archive/sf_main.html

MIT Science Fiction Society Homepage The world's largest on-line collection of science fiction texts.
http://www.mit.edu:8001/activities/mitsfs/homepage.html

New World Web Ring A series of linked Web sites featuring original science fiction.
http://www.geocities.com/Area51/2403/nwr.htm

Science Fiction, Fantasy and Horror Book Database "A collection of books, synopses, reviews, and author biographies from the science fiction, fantasy, and horror genres."
http://books.ratatosk.org/

SFF Net Good collection of links to e-zines, authors, and other sites.
http://www.sff.net/sff/index.htp

Stefan Petersson's SF&Fantasy Page A very good collection of links to other sci-fi, fantasy, and horror fiction resources on the Net.
http://julmara.ce.chalmers.se/stefan/WWW/Cyberlinks/saifai.html

Spiff's World of Science Fiction and Fantasy Another good list of authors, books, other lists, and Web pages devoted to sci-fi and fantasy.
http://http.tamu.edu:8000/~sdd2252/Docs/SciFi/SciFi.html

HORROR FICTION RESOURCES

DarkEcho's Web Authors, reviews, resources, and other information pertaining to horror fiction.
http://w3.gwis.com/~prlg/

Dracula Bram Stoker's classic, converted to e-text.
http://www.cs.cmu.edu/Web/People/rgs/drac-table.html

Fiona's Fear and Loathing Snazzy page devoted to horror literature.
http://www.oceanstar.com/horror/

RESOURCES FOR HORROR, SCIENCE FICTION, AND FANTASY WRITERS

Clique of the Tomb Beetle Horror and sci-fi zine.
http://www.tyrell.net/~rmcheal/

HorrorNet If you like Clive Barker, you'll love this site.
http://www.horrornet.com/

Transversions Magazine of speculative fiction, science fiction, fantasy, and horror.
http://www.astro.psu.edu/users/harlow/transversions/

For Writers Only An on-line workshop for writers of science fiction and fantasy.
http://www.webwitch.com/writers/

Writer's (Stumbling) Block Resources for horror, fantasy, and sci-fi writers.
http://indigo.ie/~imago/writer.html

Pegasus Online Writer's Corner Resources for the sci-fi and fantasy writer.
http://www.pegasusonline.com/writers-corner/ref-books.html

USENET NEWSGROUPS

The following Usenet newsgroups cover science fiction, fantasy, and horror fiction. Other newsgroups relating to particular authors may be found in the "Authors" section of this resource list.

alt.books.brian-lumley
alt.books.clive-barker
alt.books.dean-koontz
alt.books.deryni
alt.books.larry-niven
alt.books.m-lackey
alt.books.phil-k-dick
alt.dragons-inn
alt.fan.dragonlance
alt.drwho.creative
alt.fan.dune
alt.fan.heinlein
alt.fan.philip-dick
alt.fan.piers-anthony
alt.fan.pratchett
alt.fandom.cons
alt.fantasy.conan
alt.folklore.ghost-stories
alt.history.what-if
alt.horror

alt.horror.creative
alt.horror.cthulhu
alt.horror.werewolves
alt.tv.x-files.creative
alt.vampyres
rec.arts.sf.announce
rec.arts.sf.fandom
rec.arts.sf.marketplace
rec.arts.sf.misc
rec.arts.sf.reviews
rec.arts.sf.science
rec.arts.sf.written
rec.arts.sf.written.robert-jordan
rec.arts.startrek.reviews

ON-LINE SERVICES

The WELL: Science Fiction Conference
"The WELL Science Fiction Conference is a place for readers, writers, and others to discuss any and all aspects of speculative fiction in print and media."

America Online: SF Forum (keyword: fictional realm)

Theater Resources

Whether you're an actor, a playwright, a drama student, or just an avid theatergoer, the Internet is becoming a great place to find information about any aspect of the stage. Be sure to check Yahoo! (**http://www.yahoo.com**) for new resources.

Aisle Say The Internet magazine of stage reviews and opinion.
http://www.escape.com/~theanet/AisleSay.html

The Dramatic Exchange Site dedicated to archiving and distributing scripts.
http://www.dramex.org/

Joe Geigel's Favorite Theatre-Related Resources Very good directory of resources on the Net.
http://artsnet.heinz.cmu.edu/OnBroadway/links/

Guide to Theater Resources on the Internet From France, an extensive list of theater resources, including information on theater-related mailing lists. In English.
http://www.ircam.fr/divers/theatre-e.html

Literary Resources/Theater and Drama An excellent list maintained by Jack Lynch at the University of Pennsylvania.
http://www.english.upenn.edu/~jlynch/Lit/theatre.html

New Dramatists Home Page New Dramatists, founded in 1949, provides a variety of resources to playwrights.
http://www.itp.tsoa.nyu.edu/~diana/ndintro.html

Off Broadway Directory of current shows.
http://artsnet.heinz.cmu.edu:80/OnBroadway

Playbill On-line On-line magazine of the New York theater community.
http://www.playbill.com

Theatre Central Theater companies, playwrights, writing resources, and more, all neatly cataloged.
http://www.theatre-central.com

USENET NEWSGROUPS

rec.arts.theatre
rec.arts.theatre.misc
rec.arts.theatre.musical
rec.arts.theatre.plays

ON-LINE SERVICES

The WELL: The Theater Conference
Offers discussions on theater, opera, and performance art.

Women's Literary Resources

For many years the Internet was known as an overwhelmingly male domain, but the on-line world is changing rapidly. The women's movement in general, and women's studies programs at universities in particular, have begun to take advantage of the potential of the Net for disseminating information and analysis and building virtual communities of feminist writers and scholars.

One of the best sites devoted to women's literature gives a broad overview of what's available on the Net:

Celebration of Women Writers Links to many authors and feminist texts.

http://www.cs.cmu.edu/Web/People/mmbt/women/writers.html

Other notable sites include:

Atlantis A women's studies journal.
http://serf.msvu.ca/atlantis/

Bluejean Magazine produced by and for young women.
http://www.bluejeanmag.com/

Brown Women Writers Project Focusing on women's writing from roughly 1330 to 1830.
http://www.stg.brown.edu/projects/wwp/wwp_home.html

Diotima: Materials for Study of Women and Gender in the Ancient World
http://www.uky.edu/ArtsSciences/Classics/gender.html

Feminism and Women's Studies (Carnegie-Mellon English Server) An extraordinarily comprehensive collection of links to women's studies resources.
http://english-www.hss.cmu.edu/Feminism.html

Magazines and Newsletters on the Web (Women Focused)
http://www.library.wisc.edu/libraries/WomensStudies/mags.htm

The Orlando Project History of women's writing in Britain.
http://www.ualberta.ca/ORLANDO/

Women's Cybrary Links to books, literature, and on-line resources.
http://www.womenbooks.com/

Women's Wire On-line magazine focusing on women's resources.
http://www.women.com/

The Poetry of Sappho (7th–6th century B.C.)
http://www.sappho.com/poetry/sappho.htm

The Kassandra Project An introduction to German women writers, artists, and thinkers from the second half of the 18th century through the first decades of the 19th.
http://www.reed.edu/~ccampbel/tkp/

Victorian Women Writers Project Women writers of the late 19th century; offers background and links to works.
http://www.indiana.edu/~letrs/vwwp/

Women's Books Online Reviews of women's books.
http://www.cybergrrl.com/review/

Women's Studies WWW Pages and Gophers A selection of links to women's studies resources.
http://www-unix.umbc.edu/~korenman/wmst/links.html

Women's Studies Hotlist Dozens of well-organized links.
http://www.nau.edu/~wst/access/hotlist/hotlist.html

E-TEXTS

BOOKS ON-LINE

The following are archives of e-texts, digital versions of entire books, usually classics not covered by copyright and thus in the public domain. Simply because a book is in the public domain, though, doesn't mean that it is commonplace, and many of the texts in these archives are lesser-known works of famous authors or "forgotten classics" of bygone eras. Several archives also contain digitized versions of hard-to-find Greek and Roman classics.

Unfortunately, space considerations forbid listing every one of the thousands of e-texts available on-line here, but all of these archives are well organized and many provide search facilities, so finding particular e-texts is a remarkably simple process. If you do have difficulty finding a particular text, posting a query in the **alt.etext** Usenet newsgroup will usually bring help. It's a good idea to check **alt.etext** periodically anyway—announcements of new on-line offerings are often given there, and many writers post their own original e-texts to this group.

The e-texts in these archives are available for downloading to your home computer at no cost. It's a good idea, however, to give some thought to how long the work may be before you begin downloading it: *Crime and Punishment* might take several hours (possibly days) to transfer to your home computer, and you'd probably be far better off buying a copy at a bookstore.

Probably the best place to look for e-texts is the Project Gutenberg Home Page, where you'll find an index of the thousands of works converted to e-text by the project at **http://www.promo.net/pg/**

Other general sources of e-texts include:

Alex: A Catalog of Electronic Texts on the Internet
http://www.lib.ncsu.edu/stacks/alex-index.html

B&R Samizdat Express Publishes "Internet on a Disk," a free newsletter announcing new e-texts on the Net. The place to look for out-of-the-ordinary e-texts.
http://www.samizdat.com/

Banned Books On-line A special exhibit of books that have been the objects of censorship and censorship attempts. Many of the books themselves are available here.
http://www.cs.cmu.edu/People/spok/banned-books.html

Bibliomania A very well organized site featuring fiction, nonfiction, and reference works.
http://www.bibliomania.com/

Book Stacks Library A collection of e-texts from other archives.
http://www.books.com/lib1.htm

Center for Electronic Text and Images Includes collections focusing on Shakespeare, women's studies, and the occult.
http://www.library.upenn.edu/etext/

The Eden Etext Archive A highly subjective personal archive reflecting the page owner's tastes. You'll find everything from Aesop's Fables to an episode guide for the Muppets TV show here.
http://eden.apana.org.au/etext/

Electronic Texts, Journals, Newsletters, Magazines and Collections A good overview of e-text resources available at various sites on the Net.
http://dewey.lib.ncsu.edu/stacks/index.html

Electronic Text Center—University of Virginia Links to thousands of e-texts in a variety of languages.
http://etext.lib.virginia.edu/

The ETEXT Archives One of the most comprehensive text archives on the Net. Electronic books, zines, and informational files on a wide variety of subjects are available.
http://www.etext.org/

European Literature Lists Internet sources for literary texts in Western European languages other than English.
http://www.lib.virginia.edu/wess/etexts.html

Internet Public Library (IPL) A collection of public-domain works organized on the model of a "real" library.
http://ipl.sils.umich.edu/

The Online Books Page Links to more than 5,000 works.
http://www.cs.cmu.edu/books.html

Oxford Text Archive Many obscure and rare classical texts. Check Web page for access limitations and catalog information.
http://users.ox.ac.uk/~archive/

Project Bartleby The beginnings of a first-class on-line library of e-texts, from Columbia University.
http://www.columbia.edu/acis/bartleby/

World-Wide Web Virtual Library Links to all sorts of book-related resources, including a variety of sites offering on-line e-texts.
http://www.w3.org/hypertext/DataSources/bySubject/Overview.html

WWW VL: Literature/World Literature
http://sunsite.unc.edu/ibic/IBIC-World-Lit.html

More specialized collections of e-texts are available at:

Bhaktivedanta Book Trust Eastern religion texts.
http://www.webcom.com/~ara/col/books/

Camelot Project Arthurian texts.
http://rodent.lib.rochester.edu/camelot/cphome.htm

Carrie A collection of classic electronic texts.
http://www.ukans.edu/carrie/carrie_main.html

Christian Classics Ethereal Library
http://ccel.wheaton.edu/

CELT Irish Manuscript Project Historical Irish texts.
http://www.ucc.ie/celt/

Secular Web Atheist and related literature.
http://www.infidels.org/

Literature, Arts, and Medicine Database A database of texts relevant to humanities education for medical students.
http://mchip00.med.nyu.edu/lit-med/lit-med-db/topview.html

Marx-Engels Archive Well-organized archive of their major works.
http://csf.Colorado.EDU/psn/marx/

USENET NEWSGROUPS

alt.etext
alt.hypertext
bit.listserv-gutnberg-l

COMMERCIAL E-TEXT PUBLISHERS AND DISTRIBUTORS

Several Web sites devoted to selling copyrighted (and sometimes public-domain) e-texts on-line have emerged in the last few years:

BiblioBytes Some original works, but also charges for texts available for free elsewhere on the Net.
http://www.bb.com/

Digital Books
http://www.digitalbooks.com/

Pulpless.com Features both free original works and low-priced novels available for downloading.
http://www.pulpless.com/

Bylines A project of IRE, the National Organization of Investigative Reporters and Editors, and NICAR, the National Center for Computer-Assisted Reporting. Download high-quality fiction and nonfiction for from 50¢ for short pieces to $1.99 for novels.
http://www.bylines.org/

HYPERTEXT LITERATURE

Hypertext—text with embedded links that allow the reader to jump to another document or resource—is literally the foundation of the World Wide Web. While hypertext technology thus far has been used primarily to link sites, an increasing number of hypertext novels and other hypertext literature is starting to appear on the Web. Hypertext literature uses links to create a genuinely new, nonlinear structure for storytelling, permitting multiple paths through a narrative. All of which just proves how hard it is to describe hypertext—better to start up your Web browser and give the future a whirl. Probably the best place to begin your exploration is a page designed specifically as an introduction to hypertext:

Hyperizons: Hypertext Fiction Offers many pointers to both the theory and the practice of hypertext.
http://www.duke.edu/~mshumate/hyperfic.html

Once you get your feet wet, pay a visit to some examples of hypertext in action:

Eastgate Systems A leading publisher of both hypertext books and hypertext construction software. Their Web site offers samples of hypertext books and free trial software.
http://www.eastgate.com/

My Name is Scribe Collaborative hypertext fiction.
http://www.tmn.com/0h/Artswire/interactive/www/scibe/story.html

Twelve Blue Hypertext story by Michael Joyce.
http://www.eastgate.com/TwelveBlue/Welcome.html

The Two River View Hypertext poetry journal.
http://www.daemen.edu/pages/rlong/tworiver/

USENET NEWSGROUP

alt.hypertext

BOOKSTORES AND PUBLISHERS

BOOKSTORES

The bookstores listed here accept orders via e-mail, and some also have facilities for taking credit card orders through their Web pages. If you're looking for a particularly obscure or out-of-print book and can't find it at one of these on-line sites, post a request in the **rec.arts.books.marketplace** Usenet newsgroup.

Probably the best place to look for general information about booksellers on the Net is:

CIBON "Comprehensive Independent Booksellers On-line Network" Links to over 4,500 booksellers, many of whom have Web pages.
http://www.ambook.org/bookstores/

Other general indexes of bookstores on-line include:

Bookseller Lists
http://www.bookweb.org/bookstores/

BookWire "The First Place to Look for Book Information." Well, one of the first places, anyway. Includes a list of on-line bookstores and publishers.
http://www.bookwire.com/

The World-Wide Web Virtual Library: Publishers/Bookstores Another good list of on-line booksellers.
http://www.comlab.ox.ac.uk/archive/publishers/bookstores.html

Some specific bookstore sites you might like to visit include:

Advanced Book Exchange A wonderful site if you're looking for an out-of-print book. Search the inventories of more than 1,000 used book dealers around the U.S.
http://www.abebooks.com/

Amazon Books Claims to carry 1.1 million titles and features a handy personal notification service, which will keep you abreast of new titles in your fields of interest.
http://www.amazon.com/

Australian Online Bookstore
http://www.bookworm.com.au/

Barnes and Noble The 800-pound gorilla of bookstore chains, now on-line. Their snazzy site features reviews and author interviews.
http://www.barnesandnoble.com/

Basement Full of Books New books, available by mail directly from their authors.
http://www.sff.net/bfob/

Black Bird Mysteries Extensive inventory, on-line ordering.
http://blackbird-mysteries.com/

Blackwell's Bookshops "England's finest academic bookseller." On-line search of their huge catalog is available.
http://www.blackwell.co.uk/bookshops/

The Bookplex A chatty bookstore/resource site that seems to want to remind customers of a shopping mall.
http://www.gigaplex.com/books/index.htm

Books and Book Collecting Nice site for the collector, with links to search services and bookstores.
http://www2.gol.com/users/steve/f_books.htm

Booktraders Large used paperback bookstore.
http://www.xenoscience.com/bt/

Bookzone A very good on-line bookstore. Browse their electronic aisles or search for books by keyword. You can also enter your zip code and search for an old-fashioned "physical" bookstore in your area—they'll even draw you a map of how to get there.
http://www.bookzone.com/

Borders Books On-line site of the national chain features a searchable database of reviews.
http://www.borders.com/

A Clean Well-Lighted Place for Books Web site of a small chain of bookstores in California. Read book reviews by the stores' staffs, post your own comments, or just browse the catalog.
http://www.bookstore.com/

Cody's Books On-line home of the justifiably famous independent bookstore in Berkeley, California. On-line search of their 140,000-book catalog. Book lists and staff suggestions for both adults and children.
http://www.codysbooks.com/

The Internet Book Shop Claims a "virtual inventory" of more than 780,000 books. This really just means that they'll order anything you want, but since they're in the U.K., this is the place to look for books from Britain.
http://www.bookshop.co.uk/

Kenny's Bookshop Home Page A wonderful bookshop in Galway, Ireland. Their sophisticated search engine will find books you never knew existed.
http://www.iol.ie/resource/kennys/

Literate Traveller Specializing in travel and guide books.
http://www.literatetraveller.com/

Mysterious Galaxy Science fiction, fantasy, mystery, suspense, and horror.
http://www.mystgalaxy.com/

The Native Book Centre Offers Native American books and related materials for order on-line.
http://www.nativebooks.com/

Page One Books Independent bookstore in Albuquerque, New Mexico.
http://www.page1book.com/

The Tattered Cover Considered by many to be the best independent bookstore in the U.S.
http://www.tatteredcover.com/tc/

Solar Light An independent bookstore in San Francisco.
http://www.san-fran.com/solarlight/

Virtual Moe's The on-line home of an independent bookstore in Berkeley, California.
http://www.moesbooks.com/

Virtual WordsWorth Superbly designed home page of a discount bookseller in Cambridge, Massachusetts. Offers catalog search, on-line events, discussion areas, extensive links to other book-related sites, and more.
http://www.wordsworth.com/

USENET NEWSGROUPS

rec.arts.books
rec arts.books.marketplace

Publishers

Most major (and many smaller) publishers now have at least a basic Web page on-line. Many allow you to search their catalogs, and several will invite you to browse sample chapters of their current bestsellers. Some general indexes of publishers on-line include:

Bookwire Index of Publishers Links to more than 600 publishers, neatly indexed.
http://www.bookwire.com/index/publishers.html

Publishers' Catalogs Home Pages A comprehensive list of publishers worldwide.
http://www.lights.com/publisher/

The Small Press Net A list of links to small presses.
http://www.salzmann.com/gutter/spn.html

Just about any publisher, large or small, can be found on one of the above indexes.

For a sense of what a few of the larger publishers are up to on-line, pay a visit to some of these sites:

Bantam Doubleday Dell Online
http://www.bdd.com/

Houghton Mifflin
http://www.hmco.com/

Little, Brown
http://www.littlebrown.com/

McGraw-Hill
http://www.mcgraw-hill.com/

Oxford University Press
http://www.oup.co.uk

Penguin Books
http://www.penguin.com/usa/

Princeton University Press
http://pup.princeton.edu/

Random House
http://www.randomhouse.com/

Simon & Schuster
http://www.simonsays.com

For a sample of some of the more unusual publishers on-line, try a visit to these:

Blue Heron Publishing Children's books and books about writing.
http://www.teleport.com/~bhp/

Cedar Bay Press Publishes *Literary Fragments* magazine, nonfiction and fiction by new authors.
http://www.teleport.com/~cedarbay/index.html

Circlet Press Publishes erotic science fiction and fantasy.
http://www.apocalypse.org/circlet/home.html

Coyote Cowboy Company Humorous poetry and prose by Baxter Black, the cowboy poet.
http://www.ReadersNdex.com/coyote

Gutter Press Publishes "dangerous fiction and radical literature."
http://www.salzmann.com/gutter/

Nolo Press Publishes self-help legal reference works.
http://www.nolo.com/

Pinon Publishing Company Humor books. Publishers of *Beginning Farming* and *What Makes a Sheep Tick.*
http://readersndex.com/pinon/

Spunk Press Publishers of anarchist books, etc.
http://www.cwi.nl/cwi/people/Jack.Jansen/spunk/Spunk_Home.html

Zino Press Children's Books Publishers of high-quality rhyming and multicultural books designed to teach kindness and tolerance.
http://www.ku.com/zino1.html

E-zines, Magazines, and Newspapers

BOOK REVIEWS

Book reviews, like everything else on the Net, vary widely in quality and scope. Some are on-line versions of print publications, others are the informal collective efforts of Net book lovers, and at least one on-line review consists entirely of the opinions of a lone, albeit well-read, book lover. Many on-line book reviews welcome submissions—just check the site itself for instructions. Of course, you can always join hundreds of your fellow

Netters and post your review to the **rec.arts.books.reviews** or **alt.books.reviews** Usenet newsgroups.

Barcelona Review of Contemporary Fiction "An electronic bimonthly review dedicated to bringing you the best of international cutting-edge fiction in English/Spanish bilingual format."
http://www.web-show.com/Barcelona/Review/

Book Page On-line reviews and author interviews.
http://www.bookpage.com/

The Boston Book Review An excellent Web version of a prestigious print literary review. Search by title, author, or subject.
http://www.bookwire.com/bbr/bbr-home.html

Danny Yee's Book Reviews Hundreds of book reviews, all by Danny Yee. Danny reads a lot.
http://www.anatomy.su.oz.au/danny/book-reviews/index.html

Hungry Mind Home Page An excellent independent book review from the bookstore of the same name in St. Paul, Minnesota. Offers reviews, discussion areas, a newsletter, and lots more. One of the best sites on the Web, period.
http://www.bookwire.com/hmr/homepage.html

Independent Reader Recommended books in a wide variety of categories, picked by independent bookstores across the U.S.
http://www.independentreader.com/

New York Times Book Review Current reviews plus a searchable archive of 50,000 reviews dating back to 1980. There's also a very popular on-line discussion forum where you can hang out with other book lovers.
http://www.nytimes.com/books/home/

Notes in the Margin Reviews and criticism by one dedicated reader.
http://www.geocities.com/Athens/Forum/4148/

The Quarterly Black Review of Books Excellent Web version of a print review focusing on fiction, nonfiction, and poetry of special interest to the African-American community.
http://www.bookwire.com/qbr/qbr.html

Reviews from the Forbidden Planet Reviews of sci-fi and fantasy books.
http://www.maths.tcd.ie/mmm/index.html

Washington Post Chapter One Read the first chapter of new books and reviews and other features, then discuss it all in a very lively on-line forum. A great site.
http://www.washingtonpost.com/wp-srv/style/longterm/books/books.htm

Web del Sol Literary Complex Stylish site that showcases material from other literary reviews.
http://www.webdelsol.com/solhome.htm

WWW VL: Literature/IBIC Virtual Review of Books A collection of links to both general-interest and specialized book reviews available on-line.
http://sunsite.unc.edu/ibic/IVRB.html

USENET NEWSGROUPS

alt.books.reviews
rec.arts.books.reviews

E-zines and Literary Journals

E-zines on the Net range from the absolutely fascinating to the utterly puzzling. Fortunately, there are an enormous number of e-zines from which to choose, and new ones crop up every day on the Net. Probably the best starting point for a journey into zine-land is:

John Labovitz's E-zine-list Considered the best index of e-zines on-line.
http://www.meer.net/~johnl/e-zine-list/index.html

Other good indexes of e-zines can be found at:

Electronic Journals
http://www.edoc.com/ejournal/

Electronic Magazines Neatly catalogs hundreds of e-zines.
http://www.etext.org/Zines/

E-Zine Reviews
http://sunsite.unc.edu/faint/eziner/index.html

FactSheet Five Web site of a well-known index of print zines.
http://www.factsheet5.com

The e-zine explosion has brought with it a profusion of on-line literary journals, in many cases combining the irreverent sensibility of an e-zine with a focus on literature and writing. The following list is a sampling of some of the hundreds of literary zines on-line. Many of these journals welcome submissions from readers—check the particular site for details.

In general, e-zines are aimed at a young, "avant-pop" audience, so many mix original stories and poems, book and record reviews, and critiques of popular culture with political tracts of a vaguely anarchist bent. Many e-zines are also laden with large graphics, which can make loading them into your browser a painfully slow process, so you may wish to set your browser to "no graphics" before you start exploring.

Abraxus Reader A "reader-customizable" site: visitors choose what they want to see on subsequent visits. Fiction, poetry, etc. Accepts submissions.
http://www.nwlink.com/~vidiot/abraxus/

The Acid-Free Paper Fine art, literature, and Net culture. Welcomes submissions. A graphically elaborate site (which is a nice way of saying that it takes forever to load in your browser).
http://acid-free.simplenet.com

AfterNoon Fiction, poetry, and plays.
http://motley-focus.com/~timber/afternoon.html

Alt-X The *Utne Reader* called it "an insurgent cell in the heart of the vast digicosmos of corporate info-spamming and vapid techno-babble," but judge for yourself. Offers poetry, fiction, and essays. Another graphically elaborate

site, but there's a text-only version available for the impatient.
http://www.altx.com/

American Newspeak "A weekly satirical e-zine celebrating the Orwellian face of the 1990s with cutting-edge advances in the art of doublespeak carefully scavenged from the back pages of our finer newspapers." A great site—funny and horrifying at the same time.
http://www.scn.org/news/newspeak/

Anathema "Anathema is a magazine dedicated to writing inspired by madness. Strong language may be used in the stories."
http://www.vulliamy.demon.co.uk/anathema/

Art Bin From Sweden, with an emphasis on art and essays on art.
http://www.art-bin.com

Asphalt Strawberry (Formerly known as Change Magazine)
http://www.woodwind.com/imaja/Change/asphaltstrawberry.html

Bad Subjects Political and cultural criticism, in an Althussarian vein.
http://eng.hss.cmu.edu/bs/

Bakunin "A literary magazine for the dead Russian anarchist in all of us." Fiction, poetry, and essays, with a nondoctrinaire leftist bent. Accepts submissions.
http://www.coyote-arts.org/bakunin/

Basilisk Quarterly on-line journal of film, architecture, philosophy, literature, and music. A beautifully designed site. Content tends toward the scholarly.
http://swerve.basilisk.com/

Beatrice Nonfiction, essays, book reviews.
http://www.beatrice.com/contents/

beatthief Showcases "plagiarism, shoplifting, blackmail, and perjury." All in the name (and form) of poetry, of course.
http://www.beatthief.com/

Black Raven "A magazine of myth and symbolic studies."
http://www.motley-focus.com/~timber/raven.html

blood & aphorisms A serious on-line journal of fiction. Accepts submissions and awards prizes.
http://www.interlog.com/~fiction/

Blue Moon Review A high-quality literary fiction and poetry journal. Accepts submissions, but the competition is stiff.
http://www.thebluemoon.com/

Brazen Orality Largely poetry, evidently fueled by far too much caffeine. "Submissions of any and all stripes are encouraged, foamingly so in fact, but that's altogether up to you."
http://www.infobahnos.com/~brazen/

Breakfast Surreal Bills itself as "The Mutating Online Journal of Modern Poetry." Actually a list of links

to poetry on other people's home pages. No longer accepting new links, but still an interesting collection.
http://www.indirect.com/user/warren/surreal.html

Brink Conceptual poetry. An acquired taste. Accepts submissions.
http://brink.com/brink/

Bunnyhop On-line edition of a print zine.
http://www.bunnyhop.com/contents.html

Caffeine Magazine Fiction, poetry, and essays with a Beat bent. Offers a handy form to upload your own creations.
http://hallucinet.com/caffeine

Crank Interesting Web site of a high-profile print zine.
http://www.crank.com/

CrossConnect A fairly straight triannual electronic journal for contemporary art and writing based at the University of Pennsylvania in Philadelphia. Accepts submissions.
http://tech1.dccs.upenn.edu/~xconnect/

DargonZine Collaborative fantasy fiction by aspiring writers. Submissions are encouraged (after all, they're the whole point of this zine).
http://www.shore.net/~dargon/

dEPARTUREfROMnORMAL Putting it mildly. Short fiction and lots of artwork. Welcomes submissions.
http://www.xwinds.com/dfn/dfn.html

Depth Probe "A Web-zine about modern culture in America." Hint: They're not thrilled with it. Essays on a variety of subjects.
http://www.atdesign.com/at/Studios/Eyzaguirre/

Disgrunt A journal of unpopular opinions.
http://www.teleport.com/~damcarr/disgrunt/page1.htm

Edifice of Writing and Literature A very stylish site. Publishes theme issues (sci-fi, GenX), so check writers' guidelines before submitting material.
http://www-leland.stanford.edu/~lmgorbea/

Enormous Sky Poetry, prose, artwork, and photography produced by the students of Temple University.
http://newsrm01.main.temple.edu/sky/index.html

Enterprise City A virtual city that visitors can explore while reading snippets of fiction along the way. Hours of wandering fun, if you have the time.
http://www.rhapsodypress.com/enterprise/city.htm

Enterzone Poetry, fiction, essays.
http://ezone.org:1080/ez/

E-scape "The digital journal of speculative fiction." Publishes science fiction, fantasy, and horror. Submissions welcome. Magazine is in Adobe PDF format, requiring Acrobat reader software, available free at site.
http://www.interink.com/escape.html

eScene Yearly anthology of the "best on-line-published short fiction" from other e-zines on the Internet. Available in a variety of formats (PDF, ASCII, etc.). Submissions not accepted—work must be published elsewhere first.
http://www.etext.org/Zines/eScene/

EWG Presents Electronic Writers Group A Journal of Contemporary Thought and Fiction.
http://members.aol.com/ewgroup100/index.htm

15 Credibility Street Original fiction, poetry, and artwork. Considered one of the best Web sites. Accepts submissions.
http://www.smith.edu/15cst/

The Fray Well-designed site focusing on personal expression.
http://www.fray.com/

Fugue University of Idaho literary digest. Fiction, poetry, and interviews. Features high-profile writers, but welcomes submissions.
http://www.uidaho.edu/LS/Eng/Fugue

Gargoyle Magazine The student-run humor magazine of the University of Michigan. Welcomes submissions.
http://www.pub.umich.edu/garg/index.html

Geekgirl "The world's first cyberfeminist zine." Essays and interviews.
http://www.next.com.au/spyfood/geekgirl/

Gerbil A quarterly "Queer culture zine." Prose, poetry, fiction, nonfiction, and interviews.
http://www.multicom.org/gerbil/gerbil.htm

Glimmer Train Press Web site of a quarterly print short story journal. Some stories available on-line.
http://glimmertrain.com/

Gothic Journal The Web site of a print "news and review magazine for readers, writers, and publishers of romantic suspense, romantic mystery, and gothic, supernatural, and woman-in-jeopardy romance novels." Woman-in-jeopardy novels? Reviews, sample articles available on-line.
http://gothicjournal.com/romance/

Grilled Pterodactyl A one-man production—periodic ruminations on life, computers, and all the rest from a longtime fanzine publisher in Australia.
http://www.ozemail.com.au/~drgrigg/ptero.html

Harvard Advocate Home Page High-caliber poetry, fiction, and essays. Accepts submissions.
http://hcs.harvard.edu:80/~advocate/

Hawk A quarterly journal of art and writing. Snazzy graphics.
http://www.cruzio.com/~hawk/

Highbeams Literary quarterly from Beloit College. Submissions welcome.
http://stu.beloit.edu/~highbe/

i like monkeys Short, unusual stories. Submissions welcome.
http://thumper.pomona.edu/~parango/monkeys/

Interbang Poetry, fiction, articles, and essays, and they'd like to see yours, too. An "interbang," it seems, is a combination of a question mark and an exclamation point, and is said to be a typical reaction to the articles here.
http://www.interbang.net/

InterText: Online Fiction Magazine One of the oldest zines on-line (1991). Publishes both general fiction and science fiction/horror. Submissions welcome.
http://ftp.etext.org/Zines/InterText/intertext.html

Konzepte New writing in German, from Berlin.
http://www.cs.tu-berlin.de/~nop/konzepte/

Kudzu: A Digital Quarterly An excellent on-line review offering literary fiction, poetry, and essays. Accepts submissions.
http://www.etext.org/Zines/Kudzu/

Kyosaku "Kyosaku is a quarterly publication dedicated to fostering a healthy zeal for poetry, humor, beauty, and life in an age when many are all too prepared to shove Art's fat ass out the door and curl up with dopey New Age shinola or turn on Hard Copy." Can't argue with that. A delightfully silly zine.
http://www.cs.oberlin.edu/students/djacobs/kyo/kyomain.html

Literary Times The Web site of a print magazine that reviews romantic fiction. Not much content, but lovely pictures of flowers.
http://www.tlt.com/

Living Poets E-journal of an e-mail poetry society in Derby, England. Submissions via e-mail group; information on the Web page.
http://dougal.derby.ac.uk/lpoets/

Mississippi Review An on-line monthly magazine publishing the best of literary fiction, poetry, essays, commentary, and reviews. Winner of the 1995 GNN Best of the Net Award in Literature.
http://sushi.st.usm.edu/mrw/

Missouri Review From the University of Missouri, a serious Web literary review, offering reviews, essays, fiction, and poetry. Submissions welcome.
http://www.missouri.edu/~moreview/

Morpo Review An excellent creative Web review, featuring fiction, poetry, reviews, and more, including on-line literary discussions.
http://morpo.com/

Open Scroll Publishes short fiction and poetry "in the pursuit of passion, brilliance, and insanity." Submissions welcome.
http://www.scroll.com

Oyster Boy Review A literary magazine published in Chapel Hill, N.C. Fiction, poetry, and essays.
http://sunsite.unc.edu/ob/

Pif Well-designed Web zine showcasing new fiction and poetry, most of it, unfortunately, very bad. Submissions welcome.
http://www.dimax.com/pif/

Postmodern Culture Full text of journal of scholarly literary criticism; issues dating back to 1990 are available on-line. Sample theme: "Dynamic and Thermodynamic Tropes of the Subject in Freud and in Deleuze and Guattari."
http://jefferson.village.virginia.edu/pmc/

Prism International Web edition of a print literary magazine from Canada. Fiction, poetry, and essays. Submissions welcome, cash prizes (!) awarded.
http://www.arts.ubc.ca/prism/

Proust Said That He sure did. Home base for all things Proustian, mostly essays. This site is produced by the Marcel Proust Support Group of San Francisco and has an oddly charming atmosphere.
http://www.well.com/www/vision/proust

Pug "Fact, fiction, frenzy." Fiction, nonfiction, reviews, great graphic of a pug with glowing eyes, but zine has nothing to do with dogs.
http://www.pugzine.com/

Recursive Angel Experimental poetry, fiction, and art. Welcomes submissions.
http://www.calldei.com/~recangel/

Richmond Review An excellent on-line literary magazine from the U.K. Fiction, poetry, and essays. Reviews of current books and extensive archives.
http://www.demon.co.uk/review/

The River Literary journal with a special fondness for essays on sports. Accepts submissions.
http://www.concom.com/~pparker/

RUNE—MIT Journal of Arts and Letters Poetry, art, and prose from the Massachusetts Institute of Technology.
http://www.ai.mit.edu/~spraxlo/rune/RUNE.html

Sensitive Skin Electronic Fiction and Review "The magazine of art and literature for people who just don't care about art and literature anymore!" But people here must care, since they've produced a very fine on-line edition of a serious print literary review.
http://www.bway.net/~sskin/

So Many Roads Ezine Well-produced on-line magazine of fiction and poetry. Welcomes submissions.
http://www.radiant-iguana.com/zine.htm

Sour Grapes Online Literary Magazine A well-designed and substantial literary journal. Prose, poetry, and art. Submissions welcome.
http://www.bdt.com:80/home/brianhill/created/sgolm09/contents.html

Spirals Solid, if somewhat pretentious, poetry and fiction.
http://home.earthlink.net/~spiralz/

Sponge Stands for "Simple People Opposing Never-ending Gaudy Endeavors." Evidently considers Douglas Adams a minor deity. Inexplicable.
http://olympia.ucr.edu/~sponge

Spout Poetry Magazine From Huddersfield, England. Publishes only the output of a poetry workshop there, so if you like this page, perhaps you'd best move to Huddersfield.
http://www.cs.man.ac.uk/peve/Staff/Jon/Poetry/spout.html

Standards Dedicated to promoting a multicultural analysis of society. Poetry, essays, interviews, and fiction. A visually striking site, but the actual content is a bit tedious.
http://stripe.Colorado.EDU/~standard/

Stanford Humanities Review Web site of an academic review. Interesting, if largely theoretical, content.
http://shr.stanford.edu/shreview/index.html

Stange's Nebula An interesting Web reincarnation of the defunct Canadian literary magazine *Nebula* (1975–1983). Each issue contains a single long feature. Back issues available on-line.
http://www.wp.com/nebula/

State of unBeing "A collection of thought-provoking writing and literary trash." Ratio of the latter to the former seems very high. Extensive archives of past issues available on-line.
http://www.io.com/~hagbard/sob.html

Super AM Magazine "The journal for the science of leisure and the technology of art." A mildly bizarre site, featuring poetry, prose, and fat-free recipes.
http://www.superam.com/

Swagazine Rack Fiction, poetry, and prose culled from the writings of subscribers to the Swagland BBS, a local bulletin board system in Santa Barbara, California.
http://www.silcom.com/~zeylan/swagazine/

Think Thank Thunk Art, poetry, and fiction, which they spell "fik-shun."
http://www.thinkthankthunk.com/

Treeline: Canadian Writing on the Net A beautifully produced and innovative literary magazine with high-quality content. Poetry, fiction, essays, and art. Lists current literary contests and events. A first-rate Web resource for readers and writers.
http://130.179.92.25/Treeline/Treeline.html

Trincoll Journal A weekly multimedia arts journal. Published since 1992 entirely by college students.
http://www.trincoll.edu/tj/trincolljournal.html

256 Shades of Grey Eau Claire, Wisconsin's avant-pop literary/arts zine. Accepts poetry, fiction, essays, nonfiction, music reviews, etc.
http://www.primenet.com/~blkgrnt/index.html

Unit Circle "Your one-stop alternative culture shop." Art, fiction, poetry, music, and book reviews. Submissions welcome.
http://www.etext.org:80/Zines/UnitCircle/

Urban Desires *The New York Times* calls it "one of the most polished, hippest magazines on the Web, with imaginative, often interactive, art projects." Art, fiction, cultural criticism. Always something interesting.
http://www.desires.com

Verbal Abuse Urban nihilist poetry and fiction. The outgrowth of a reading series begun in a New York City nightclub in 1993.
http://mosaic.echonyc.com/~interjackie/verbal/verbal.html

Webster's Weekly Mostly personal essays on various aspects of modern life.
http://www.awa.com/w2/

Zuzu's Petals Literary Resource One of the best sites on the Web for readers. Home of Zuzu's Petals Literary Quarterly, a high-quality Web literary review. Fiction, poetry, essays, and more—submissions encouraged. This site also offers an excellent selection of links to resources elsewhere on the Net, but there is an enormous amount of fascinating material right here. Named, incidentally, for Jimmy Stewart's daughter in *It's a Wonderful Life.*
http://www.lehigh.net/zuzu/zu-link.htm

USENET NEWSGROUPS

alt.etext
alt.zines
rec.mag.fsfnet

ON-LINE SERVICES

The WELL: Factsheet Five Conference
An electronic extension of the traditional paper magazine of the same name. A comprehensive review of the print zine scene.

Magazines

The following is a selection of Net sites established by general-interest print magazines and journals as well as general-interest magazines that exist only on the Web. The amount of the content of the print versions of print magazines that publishers choose to make available free on-line varies considerably. Some offer just a few excerpts to whet the reader's appetite, and usually include a form allowing those interested to subscribe on-line. Other magazines, for example *The Atlantic Monthly* (**http://www.theatlantic.com/**), put almost the entire contents of the print magazine on-line (and, in the case of *The Atlantic*, offer additional features to on-line browsers not found in the print version). The theory behind such apparent largesse seems to be that, since few people will actually read the entire magazine on their computer screens, putting the whole thing on-line is really the most effective way to catch a potential subscriber's attention. Almost all on-line magazines now also have begun to carry some form of advertising.

A glimpse into one possible future of magazines on the Net is afforded by *Salon* (**http://www.salonmagazine.com/**), a Web-based magazine devoted to culture and the arts. *Salon,* which is "published" on the Web daily, covers issues of substance with a liveliness and style rare in on-line publications. It also has established an on-line conferencing system where readers can discuss articles in the magazine.

The oldest repository of general interest print magazines on-line is the *Electronic Newsstand* (**http://www.enews.com/**), which offers excerpts from hundreds of print magazines (usually a few articles from the current issue), as well as subscription information. Many of the print magazines that first dipped their toes in the Net via the Electronic Newsstand have gone on to establish their own independent Web sites. An overview of magazines available on the Net, both print and Web-only, can be found at the following sites:

AJR NewsLink/Magazines
http://www.newslink.org/mag.html

Starting Point—Magazines A roundup of magazines on-line.
http://www.stpt.com/magazine.html

Ecola's Newsstand
http://www.ecola.com/news/magazine/

The following are a few notable examples of magazine Web sites. As usual, if you don't see your favorite here, it doesn't mean it doesn't exist on the Net—just search at

Yahoo! (**http://www.yahoo.com**) or one of the other search engines listed on page 127 and you may be pleasantly surprised.

Advertising Age
http://www.adage.com/

The Atlantic Monthly Most of the print magazine on-line.
http://www.theatlantic.com/

The American Prospect
http://epn.org/prospect.html

Barron's (requires paid subscription)
http://www.barrons.com/

Business Week
http://www.businessweek.com

Condé Net Online Home base for several on-line magazines, including Epicurious, a combination of the *Bon Appetit* and *Gourmet* print magazines.
http://www.cntraveler.com/

Feed High-profile on-line–only journal of arts and culture.
http://www.feedmag.com/

George John F. Kennedy Jr.'s journal of politics and opinion.
http://www.georgemag.com/toc.html

George Jr. No relation to above, just a far more interesting journal of art and culture.
http://www.georgejr.com/

Life Magazine
http://pathfinder.com/Life

Maclean's Canada's national newsweekly magazine.
http://www.macleans.ca

Paris Match
http://www.parismatch.tm.fr/

Mother Jones
http://www.mojones.com

National Geographic
http://www.nationalgeographic.com/media/ngm/index.html

New Republic
http://www.enews.com/magazines/tnr/

ONE An African-American journal of art, music, and politics.
http://www.clark.net/pub/conquest/one/home.html

The Paris Review
http://www.voyagerco.com/PR/

People Magazine
http://pathfinder.com/people/

Premiere Magazine On-line version of the entertainment magazine.
http://www.premieremag.com

Private Eye Net version of the British satirical magazine.
http://www.intervid.co.uk/intervid/eye/gateway.html

Readers' Digest Humor In Uniform On-line!
http://www.readersdigest.com/

Redbook
http://homearts.com/rb/toc/00rbhpc1.htm

Slate Microsoft's on-line journal of politics and culture. By subscription ($30/yr.) only.
http://www.slate.com

Smithsonian Magazine
http://www.smithsonianmag.si.edu/

Der Spiegel German news magazine (in German).
http://www.spiegel.de/

Sports Illustrated
http://www.pathfinder.com/si/welcome.html

Suck Irreverent and often inexplicable cultural commentary.
http://www.suck.com

Time Magazine
http://time.com/index.html

Time Warner Pathfinder Gateway to a variety of Time Warner magazines.
http://www.pathfinder.com

US News Online From U.S. News and World Report Inc.
http://www.readersdigest.com/

The Utne Lens Web site of the *Utne Reader* magazine.
http://www.utne.com/lens/

Wired Magazine
http://www.hotwired.com/wired/

Word A well-designed and consistently intriguing magazine of arts and culture.
http://www.word.com/

USENET NEWSGROUP

rec.mag

ON-LINE SERVICES

In general, the on-line services' versions of popular magazines contain features, such as extensive archives of past articles, not available in the free Web versions of the same magazines.

America Online: Newsstand (keyword: newsstand)—On-line editions of dozens of magazines, from *Air Force World* to *Worth Magazine*. Best feature: The content of the magazines is searchable for articles on specific subjects.

Newspapers and Other News Sources

Browsing the Net will never be a substitute for reading a good daily newspaper, but there are a growing number of serious news journals on the Web. Even many small newspapers have established on-line editions, which can provide a valuable glimpse into the news from faraway places that may not make it into your local paper.

INDEXES OF NEWSPAPERS

AJR Newslink A comprehensive and very well organized site. Features 469 newspaper, 360 broadcast,

508 magazine, and 467 special links, plus surveys and "Top 10" lists. Produced by the *American Journalism Review*.
http://www.newslink.org/menu.html

Editor & Publisher Home Page Offers features on print media as well as a list of links to on-line newspapers.
http://www.mediainfo.com/edpub/

The European Journalism Page Links to many European publications.
http://www.demon.co.uk/eurojournalism/

LC Newspaper and Current Periodical Room Newspaper Links A comprehensive index from the U.S. Library of Congress.
http://lcweb.loc.gov/global/ncp/extnewsp.html

The Omnivore Excellent news source with links to many unusual publications.
http://way.net/omnivore/

NEWSPAPERS

The Army Times
http://www.armytimes.com/

Boston Globe
http://www.boston.com/globe/glohome.htm

The Christian Science Monitor
http://www.csmonitor.com

Daily Record and Sunday Mail From the U.K.
http://www.record-mail.co.uk/rm/drsm/front1.html

The Daily Yomiuri From Japan, in Japanese.
http://www.yomiuri.co.jp/

Detroit Free Press
http://www.freep.com/

The Electronic Telegraph—An excellent on-line newspaper from the U.K. Free, but requires registration.
http://www.telegraph.co.uk

Evening Times Online (Scotland)
http://www.eveningtimes.co.uk/

Financial Times (USA Edition)
http://www.usa.ft.com/

The Gate A joint on-line project of the *San Francisco Chronicle* and the *San Francisco Examiner*.
http://www.sfgate.com

The Guardian WebSite From the U.K.
http://www.guardian.co.uk/

The Haight Ashbury Free Press A vintage alternative newspaper published in San Francisco.
http://www.webcom.com/haight

The Hindu A popular English-language newspaper in India.
http://www.webpage.com/hindu/today/index.html

The Hollywood Reporter
http://www.hollywoodreporter.com/m.shtml

Hong Kong Standard Newspapers
http://www.hkstandard.com

The Irish Times
http://www.irish-times.com

The Jerusalem Post
http://www.jpost.co.il/

Jewish Post of New York Online
http://www.jewishpost.com/

Los Angeles Times
http://www.latimes.com/

Mercury Center Home Page *San Jose Mercury* home page.
http://www.sjmercury.com/

The NandO Times One of the oldest and best of the on-line newspapers.
http://www2.nando.net/nt/

The National Enquirer Online Not the whole paper, but about the same number of articles you'd read on the checkout line.
http://www.nationalenquirer.com/

The New York Times on the Web Free access to most of each day's issue, including classified ads.
http://www.nytimes.com

New York Daily News NYC's classic tabloid.
http://www.mostnewyork.com/

The Observer Life Magazine Supplement to the *Observer* newspaper in England.
http://www.observer.co.uk/

Our World News News from an African-American perspective.
http://www.gateway2.com/ourworldnews/

Russia Today (in English)
http://www.russiatoday.com/

The St. Petersburg Times (Russia)
http://www.spb.su/times/index.html

Telegraph of London
http://www.telegraph.co.uk/

Times of London Includes both the daily *Times* and *The Sunday Times*
http://www.the-times.co.uk/

Toronto Star
http://www.thestar.com/

USA Today Full text of the newspaper once characterized as "Television you can wrap fish in."
http://www.usatoday.com/

Wall Street Journal Interactive Edition News, features, and columnists. Subscription only ($49/yr.).
http://www.wsj.com/

Washington Post
http://www.washingtonpost.com/

The Washington Times National Weekly
http://www.washtimes-weekly.com/

OTHER SOURCES OF NEWS

Associated Press Free news briefs, updated frequently.
http://www.nytimes.com/aponline/indexNews.html

CBS News: UTTMlink "Up-to-the-minute," in case you were wondering.
http://uttm.com/

Columnists from The Washington Post Including Miss Manners.
http://wp1.washingtonpost.com/wp-srv/style/longterm/columns/columns.htm

CNN Interactive News features from the television news network.
http://www.cnn.com/

Crayon Crayon lets you design your own daily "newspaper" compiled from free on-line sources—every time you click on the Crayon bookmark in your Web browser, you get a new "edition."
http://crayon.net

DisInformation "The Subculture Search Engine" Actually a collection of articles and links explaining everything from the irradiation of our food to what William Burroughs was really talking about. Features reader forums where you can chat with all sorts of unusual folks.
http://www.disinfo.com/

Jinn Pacific News Service's biweekly on-line magazine.
http://www.pacificnews.org/jinn/

Media Online Yellow Pages A directory of media outlets and contacts.
http://www.webcom.com/~nlnnet/yellowp.html

MSNBC A joint project of Microsoft and NBC News.
http://www.msnbc.com/

NewsPage Home Page News retrieval service. Requires registration and charges a fee for full-text articles.
http://www.newspage.com/

Newsworks A collaborative on-line venture by 125 U.S. newspapers. Features articles on common themes from member papers. The result is a sort of "super on-line newspaper." You can also search the content of the member papers from one spot.
http://www.newsworks.com/

YO! (Youth Outlook) A bimonthly news journal of youth culture.
http://www.pacificnews.org/yo/

USENET NEWSGROUPS

alt.journalism
alt.journalism.criticism
alt.journalism.newspapers
alt.journalism.print

ON-LINE SERVICES

America Online: Chicago Tribune
Full text and searchable archives.

America Online: Weekly World News
Full text and archives. Full coverage of Elvis sightings, the Bat Boy, and other stories mysteriously not covered by the mainstream media.

America Online: San Jose Mercury News
Full text and searchable archives.

America Online: New York Times
Full text and searchable archives.

LIBRARIES AND REFERENCE SOURCES

Dictionaries and Other Language Resources

Inasmuch as the Internet sprang from academic roots and remains largely a written medium, the vast range of language resources available on-line is not surprising. On-line dictionaries and glossaries abound, and the Internet community's love of words and language is evidenced by the wide variety of language resources on-line.

DICTIONARIES

Hypertext Webster Interface A free on-line English dictionary.
http://c.gp.cs.cmu.edu:5103/prog/webster

On-line Dictionaries and Glossaries A good directory of what's available on-line.
http://www.rahul.net/lai/glossaries.html

Pedro's Dictionaries Links to an amazing assortment of multilingual and special dictionaries.
http://www.public.iastate.edu/~pedro/dictionaries.html

OTHER GENERAL LANGUAGE RESOURCES

Addicted to Words An examination of words in all their social roles.
http://www.morestuff.com/words/a2wdgood.htm

The Anti-Pedantry Page A lucid explanation of why "Everyone loves their cat" is grammatically correct.
http://uts.cc.utexas.edu/~churchh/austheir.html

British Slang Glossary
http://eno.princeton.edu/~ben/vocab/vocab.html

The Broken Rules Page Why "Never end a sentence with a preposition" is silly.
http://www.ojohaven.com/fun/broken.rules.html

The Cool Word of the Day Page
http://130.63.218.180/~wotd/

The Cymdeithas Madog Home Page Learn Welsh on the Web.
http://tpowel.comdis.lsumc.edu/cymraeg/madog.htm

Dave Wilton's Etymology Page
http://home.sprynet.com/sprynet/dwilton/etyma1.htm

An Elementary Grammar Help at last for the gerund-challenged.
http://www.hiway.co.uk/~ei/intro.html

The English Server at CMU An extensive and well-designed site with links to hundreds of language resources.
http://english.hss.cmu.edu/

French Slang You, you, son of a poodle, you!
http://www.easynet.co.uk/home/fslang.htm

Grammar Hotline Directory Is the question of "which or that" the one that (which?) is driving you around the bend? Here's a list of experts you can call (on the telephone), arranged by state.
http://www1.infi.net/tcc/tcresourc/faculty/dreiss/writcntr/hotline.html

Grammar and Style Notes Jack Lynch sets you straight.
http://www.english.upenn.edu/~jlynch/grammar.html

The Human-Languages Page An outstanding collection of linguistic resources, arranged by language.
http://www.june29.com/HLP/

The Jargon File—Geek Dictionary of Computing Terminology
http://www.ccil.org/jargon/jargon.html

Jesse's Word of the Day Random House dictionary editor Jesse Sheidlower answers your etymology questions.
http://www.randomhouse.com/jesse/index.cgi

The King's English H.W. Fowler's classic grammar guide.
http://www.columbia.edu/acis/bartleby/fowler/

Klingon Language Institute Phasers on stun—they're serious.
http://kli.org/

Larry's Aussie Slang and Phrase Dictionary From the Back of the Beyond.
http://www.uq.edu.au/~zzlreid/slang.html

Merriam-Webster Online A searchable dictionary and thesaurus from the dictionary publishers.
http://www.m-w.com/mw/mwhome.htm

OED News News from the folks who bring you the Oxford English Dictionary.
http://www.oup.co.uk/newoed.html

One-Look Dictionary Submits your search term to 159 separate on-line dictionaries.
http://www.onelook.com/

Online Slang Dictionaries
http://www.uwasa.fi/comm/termino/collect/slang.html

Propaganda Analysis Home Page You are what you read.
http://carmen.artsci.washington.edu/propaganda/home.htm

Twists, Slugs and Roscoes: A Glossary of Hardboiled Slang—A glossary compiled from a variety of detective novels.
http://www.vex.net/~buff/slang.html

Vietnam Veteran's Terminology and Slang
http://grunt.space.swri.edu/glossary.htm

The Weekly Idiom Each week, an explanation of a new English idiom and an accompanying sample dialogue.
http://www.comenius.com/idiom/index.html

Word for Word A dandy language column from Down Under.
http://peg.pegasus.oz.au/~toconnor/

The Word Detective A language column written by Yours Truly.
http://www.word-detective.com/

Word Play An excellent collection of links to Net sites devoted to having fun with words.
http://www.wolinskyweb.com/word.htm

Wordwatch A fascinating weekly commentary on current English.
http://titania.cobuild.collins.co.uk:80/wordwatch.html

World Wide Words Fascinating essays by Micheal Quinion.
http://clever.net/quinion/words

USENET NEWSGROUPS

alt.usage.english
bit.listserv.words-1
misc.education.language.english
sci.lang

ON-LINE SERVICES

America Online: Merriam-Webster
A good collection of useful M-W offerings, including the Merriam-Webster Bookstore, Collegiate Dictionary, Kids' Dictionary, Medical Dictionary, Thesaurus, Word Histories, and Word of the Day. Word Histories Forum features interesting discussions of word origins.

The WELL: The Words Conference
A place to discuss the vagaries, peculiarities, oddities, beauties, and inanities of language.

The WELL: Language Conference
Discussion of all aspects of human language and its role in society.

Libraries On-line

Contrary to popular impression (unfortunately), it is rarely possible to actually access the contents of books held by libraries via the Internet. You can, however, browse the catalogs of most libraries, and many libraries have extensive research materials available on-line. Many libraries also make available on-line exhibits of archival material and historical documents, such as the remarkable *American Memory* (**http://rs6.loc.gov:80/amhome.html**) exhibit mounted by the U.S. Library of Congress. Many library sites also maintain extensive lists of links to other sites of interest on the Internet.

Although many libraries are in the process of converting their catalogs to make them fully accessible via the Web, the process is slow. In many cases, library catalogs currently are available only via a telnet connection (see Chapter 3 for an explanation of how telnet works). It is common for these libraries to maintain a Web page offering general information about the library and a hypertext link to click which will then initiate a telnet session with the actual library catalog. Fortunately, you'll almost always find information about how to log in to (and log out from) the library's telnet system right there on the Web page, and with just a little practice you'll have the free run of the catalogs of the largest libraries in the world. Don't be afraid to experiment—you can't break anything.

General information about libraries on the Net and directories of libraries on-line around the world can be found at:

American Library Association Founded in 1876, this is the oldest and largest library association in the world.
http://www.ala.org/

Bookwire Directory of Libraries More than 500 libraries on-line worldwide, indexed by location and name.
http://www.bookwire.com/index/libraries.html

Library WWW Servers A worldwide directory of libraries on the Web.
http://sunsite.berkeley.edu/libweb

Literature Webliography A guide to scholarly library resources.
http://www.lib.lsu.edu/hum/lit.html

<u>Virtual Libraries on the Web</u>
http://www.w3.org/hypertext/DataSources/bySubject/Virtual_libraries/Overview.html

Specific libraries (or subject-oriented directories of libraries) worth a visit include:

<u>Association of Research Libraries</u>
http://arl.cni.org/

<u>Australian Libraries</u>
http://info.anu.edu.au/ozlib/ozlib.html

<u>Chicago Public Library</u>
http://cpl.lib.uic.edu/

<u>Gabriel</u> The information server for Europe's National Libraries.
http://portico.bl.uk/gabriel/en/welcome.html

<u>INFOMINE-UC Riverside Libraries</u>
http://lib-www.ucr.edu/

<u>Library of Congress</u>
http://lcweb.loc.gov/homepage/lchp.html

<u>National Library of Canada</u>
http://www.nlc-bnc.ca/

<u>National Library of New Zealand</u>
http://www.natlib.govt.nz/

<u>National Network of Libraries of Medicine</u>
http://www.nnlm.nlm.nih.gov/

New York Public Library Home Page
http://www.nypl.org/

Portico—The British Library
http://portico.bl.uk/

Stanford University Digital Libraries Project
http://www-diglib.stanford.edu/diglib/

The Virginia Library and Information Network
http://www.vsla.edu/

USENET NEWSGROUP

soc.libraries.talk

Reference Sources

The good news is that there are many useful reference sources available on the Net for free. The bad news is that most current editions of dictionaries and encyclopedias are covered by copyright and not available to the public on the Internet, except for the *Encyclopaedia Britannica*, available by paid subscription (see below). Some other sources are on-line, but simply not accessible to the public—the *Oxford English Dictionary*, for example, is currently available on-line only to students at universities that have paid licensing fees to Oxford University Press.

Each of the commercial on-line services offers its subscribers access to a selection of current reference works as well as more sophisticated databases. If you are planning to conduct serious research on-line, it may be worth subscribing to one of these services.

Many of the reference works that are available for free on the Net are older editions of popular works (*Bartlett's Quotations*, *Roget's Thesaurus*, etc.) now not covered by copyright and, consequently, in the public domain.

One commercial research service that you may wish to consider subscribing to is The Electric Library (**http://www.elibrary.com/**). A subscription (which includes unlimited searches via the service's Web page) is approximately $60 per year, but it gives you access to the full text (not just abstracts) of 1,578,218 newspaper articles, 309,351 magazine articles, over 167,179 book chapters, 1,103 maps, 37,979 television and radio transcripts, and all the major news agencies. A thirty-day free trial is available at the Electric Library Web site. Short of springing for a personal Nexis account (very expensive), the Electric Library is your best source of real, reliable research information on the Net.

There are several directories of free on-line reference works available on the Net. Among them:

On-line Reference Works A good roundup of reference resources.
http://www.cs.cmu.edu/Web/references.html

The Virtual Reference Desk An excellent overview of on-line reference sources from Purdue University.
http://thorplus.lib.purdue.edu/reference/index.html

The Wired Cybrarian The *Wired* magazine editors' guide to doing research on the Net. Excellent links, very well organized.
http://www.wired.com/cybrarian/

INFORMATION ABOUT THE U.S. GOVERNMENT

The U.S. federal government has made a wide variety of useful information available on-line, and other U.S. government information is available from nongovernmental Net sites such as law schools. A few notable sources of information:

Department of the Treasury IRS tax forms, assistance, and information. They'll even come to your house if you ask nicely.
http://www.irs.ustreas.gov/

Federal Bureau of Investigation
http://www.fbi.gov

U.S. Copyright Office Home Page
http://lcweb.loc.gov/copyright/

U.S. Department of Health and Human Services
http://www.os.dhhs.gov/

U.S. Patent and Trademark Office
http://www.uspto.gov/

U.S. Tax Code On-Line
http://www.fourmilab.ch/ustax/ustax.html

U.S. Trademark Law
http://www.law.cornell.edu/topics/trademark.html

The White House
http://www.whitehouse.gov/

OTHER HELPFUL REFERENCE RESOURCES

1996 CIA World Factbook Information about all the countries in the world, courtesy of the U.S. Central Intelligence Agency.
http://www.odci.gov/cia/publications/nsolo/wfb-sla.htm

AT&T Internet Toll Free 800 Directory
http://www.tollfree.att.net/dir800/

Bartlett's Familiar Quotations The 1901 edition, which actually contains many great quotations subsequently dropped from commercially published versions.
http://www.columbia.edu/acis/bartleby/bartlett/

CitySearch Excellent local information for a wide range of cities, including detailed listings of author appearances and other literary events.
http://www.citysearch.com/

Currency Converter What is that in Zlotls? Updated daily.
http://www.oanda.com/cgi-bin/ncc

Encyclopaedia Britannica Online Subscription-based: $85/year, or $8.50/mo.
http://www.eb.com/

The Intelligence Community Information about the folks who gather information about you.
http://www.odci.gov/ic/

The Internet Movie Database Everything you ever wanted to know about movies—casts, directors, etc.
http://us.imdb.com

The National Archives Information Server Home of the National Archives and Records Administration. Offers on-line searches of the Federal Register, the John F. Kennedy Assassination Records Collection, and other databases.
http://www.nara.gov/

NOAA Central Library (National Oceanic and Atmospheric Administration) A collection of more than 1 million books, journals, technical reports, microfiche, microfilm, compact disks, and databases.
http://www.lib.noaa.gov/

REFLAW A reference source for law-related issues from the Washburn University School of Law Library in Topeka, Kansas.
http://lawlib.wuacc.edu/washlaw/reflaw/reflaw.html

Roget's Thesaurus Again, an older (1911) but perhaps better version than those commercially available.
http://www.thesaurus.com/

U.S. Census Bureau Gazetteer Look up data from the 1990 U.S. Census.
http://www.census.gov/cgi-bin/gazetteer

U.S. Postal Service Zip Code Information
http://www.usps.gov/ncsc/

U.S. State Department Travel Advisories Where you don't want to go on your summer vacation.

gopher://gopher.stolaf.edu/77/.index/US-State-Department-Travel-Advisories

Vanderbilt University Television News Archive
Abstracts of all major TV newscasts since 1968(!). A remarkable project. Searchable by year and major events.
http://tvnews.vanderbilt.edu/

Yahoo! Maps You can even get door-to-door driving directions to your destination.
http://maps.yahoo.com/yahoo/

ON-LINE SERVICES

America Online: Compton's Encyclopedia
More than 35,000 articles searchable by subject or keyword.

America Online: General Reference
A variety of searchable reference works, including *National Geographic Atlas*, *The Dictionary of Cultural Literacy*, *Merriam-Webster's Collegiate Dictionary*, *Merriam-Webster's Medical Dictionary*, *The Columbia Concise Encyclopedia*, *The Macmillan Information SuperLibrary*, *Merriam-Webster's Thesaurus*, and *Merriam-Webster's Word Histories*.

WRITING RESOURCES

Something about the Internet attracts writers (it must be all those words . . .), making it a great place to find advice on writing, as well as writers' resources by the bushel. Thanks to the Net, you can even take advantage of high-powered creative writing programs at major universities through the OWLs (on-line writing laboratories) listed below. The best thing about the Net for a writer, of course, is that it's chock-full of people eager to read what you've written—many of the sites listed below welcome submissions.

General Writing Resources

Booktalk Information about publishers, agents, bookstores, and lots more. If you'd like to make a living from writing, this is an extremely helpful site. Includes a list of literary agents.
http://www.booktalk.com/

The Copyright Website Helpful hints on protecting your work.
http://www.benedict.com/

U.S. Copyright Office
http://lcweb.loc.gov/copyright/

Editorial Eye A sampler of articles from a useful print newsletter for writers.
http://www.eeicom.com/eye/

Inkspot Your one-stop guide to writing resources on the Web. A great place to start.
http://www.inkspot.com/

Online Resources for Writers A directory of Internet resources.
http://www.ume.maine.edu/~wcenter/resource.html

Poets & Writers Online A truly great site from one of the premier print writers' magazines. Many articles from the print magazine, dozens of valuable links, and even a Web-based discussion forum where you can discuss ideas (and problems) with other writers.
http://www.pw.org/

Publisher's Weekly Home Page Bestseller lists and industry news.
http://www.bookwire.com/pw/pw.html

Reader's & Writer's Resource Page A comprehensive page devoted to making life easier for writers. Many valuable links to resources elsewhere on the Net.
http://www.diane.com/readers/

Write On-Line A directory of on-line writing groups, including those available on the commercial on-line services.
http://www.writepage.com/riteline.htm

The Write Place Tools, inspiration, and resources for all kinds of writing. Opportunities for you to contribute your own writing to the page.
http://www.writepage.com/index.html

Writers Groups A listing of writing groups that meet in person.
http://www.writepage.com/groups.htm

Writers on the Net Offers a collection of services for writers and aspiring writers, including on-line classes and tutoring via e-mail.
http://www.writers.com

WritersNet Well-organized site offering tons of information for writers, editors, publishers, and agents.
http://www.writers.net/

University Writing Programs and Writing Laboratories

On-line writing labs are wonderful sources of information of use to writers—grammar guides, style manuals, resource lists, and specialized guidance on everything from how to write a research paper to the proper format for a doctoral dissertation. These pages also offer lists of links to other writing resources on the Internet.

Dakota State University Online Writing Lab (OWL)
http://www.dsu.edu:80/departments/liberal/cola/OWL/

Purdue On-Line Writing Lab (OWL)
http://owl.english.purdue.edu/

The Rensselaer Writing Center Handouts
http://www.rpi.edu/dept/llc/writecenter/web/handouts.html

Texas Undergraduate Writing Center
http://www.utexas.edu/depts/uwc/.html/handout.html

Journalism Resources

American Journalism Review A comprehensive guide to journalism resources on the World Wide Web; in-

cludes information on awards and fellowships available to journalists.
http://www.newslink.org/menu.html

Columbia Journalism Review Web site of the premier American journalism review. Features a collection of the articles and photos that won Pulitzers.
http://www.cjr.org/

Internet Newsroom "Your Guide to Electronic Fact-gathering"—how to use the resources on the Net to do research.
http://www.editors-service.com

Media Watchdog A collection of on-line media-watch resources, including specific media criticism articles and information about media-watch groups.
http://theory.lcs.mit.edu/~mernst/media/

Pulitzer Prizes A complete list of winners, by year.
http://www.pulitzer.org/

The Reporter's Internet Survival Guide An AP reporter's Internet resource list.
http://www.qns.com/~casey/

Reporters' Resource Page Another good directory of information sources on the Net.
http://www.uttm.com/reporter/

Helpful Resources for Writers

The Electric Editors Resources and mailing lists for editors and writers.
http://www.ikingston.demon.co.uk/ee/home.htm

The Elements of Style The original by William Strunk, from Columbia University's Bartleby Project.
http://www.columbia.edu/acis/bartleby/strunk/

Gender-free Pronoun Guide
http://www.lumina.net/OLD/gfp/

Grammar and Style Guides for Writers The rules of the road to success.
http://www.inkspot.com/craft/style.html

Grammar and Style Notes A very well-done guide to common grammar and style questions.
http://www.english.upenn.edu/~jlynch/grammar.html

Guide to Punctuation Your friend the semicolon.
http://sti.larc.nasa.gov/html/Chapt3/Chapt3-TOC.html

The It's vs. Its Page
http://www.rain.org/~gshapiro/its.html

Quotes for Writers
http://www.inkspot.com/craft/quotes.html

Resources for Writers and Writing Instructors A good roundup of on-line resources.
http://www.english.upenn.edu/~jlynch/writing.html

Thinking and Writing Clearly Tips on clearing the fuzz from your noggin.
http://www.midnightbeach.com/hs/clarity.htm

University of Victoria Writer's Guide A college course in writing transformed into a hypertext guidebook.

http://webserver.maclab.comp.uvic.ca/writersguide/welcome.html

Writers Write "The Internet Writing Journal."
http://www.writerswrite.com/journal/

Writers' Organizations

Academy of American Poets
http://www.poets.org/

American Society of Journalists and Authors
http://www.asja.org/

National Writers Union Home Page
http://www.nwu.org/nwu/

PEN America Center Defends freedom of expression around the world.
http://pen.org/

Poetry Society of America Oldest poetry organization in the U.S.
http://www.bookwire.com/psa/

Society of Children's Book Writers and Illustrators
http://www.scbwi.org/

Screenwriting

Hollywood Writers Network Tons of resources for the aspiring screenwriter, including chat rooms where you can swap tips with veterans.
http://www.hollywoodnetwork.com/hn/writing/

Internet Screenwriter's Network
http://www.screenwriters.com/screennet.html

Screenwriter's Heaven "Your one-stop guide to screenwriting resources around the Internet."
http://www.impactpc.demon.co.uk/

Children's Writing Resources

Children's Book Council On-line site of a trade association of children's publishers.
http://www.cbcbooks.org/

Children's Writing Resource Center A directory of on-line resources.
http://www.write4kids.com/index.html

Inkspot Resources for Children's Writers An excellent compilation of resources.
http://www.inkspot.com/genres/child.html

Diaries and Collective Writing Projects

Bad Writing Project Nothing raises the spirits like a little *schadenfreude.* No matter how bad a writer you may think you are, you'll never be this bad. Contributions welcomed.
http://www.nyx.net/~rebell/writprj.html

The Passing Show A do-it-yourself commentary on life. Visitors may add what they like.
http://www.europa.com/~kbsadler/passingshow.html

USENET NEWSGROUPS

alt.prose

alt.prose.d
misc.writing
misc.writing.screenplays

ON-LINE SERVICES

America Online:

Writers Club (keyword: writers)
Message board, chat room, file libraries, extensive resources for writers and a place to post your own on-line–writing biography.

Writers Resources (keyword: writersresources)
Grammar and style guides and the NYPL Book of 20th Century Quotations.

Books and Writing (keyword: books)
A great roundup of resources available on AOL for readers and writers.

The WELL: Byline—Freelance Writers Conference
For freelance nonfiction writers who want to swap advice on marketing themselves and their work, share information on practical business issues like health insurance and home offices, and exchange tips on research and writing.

The WELL: Media Conference
Discussion of all aspects of print and electronic journalism, with special emphasis on the legal and ethical problems facing practitioners.

The WELL: Periodical/Newsletter Conference
Publishers of newsletters and other small periodicals share resources and information.

The WELL: The Writers Conference
The large number of professional writers on The WELL make this conference a good place to find answers to questions regarding submissions, query letters, grants and awards, writers' colonies, writer's block, and the latest news from the world of publishing.

SOURCES OF INFORMATION ABOUT THE INTERNET

The best place to find news and information about the Internet is, not surprisingly, on the Internet. In fact, the Net never seems to tire of talking about itself. Below are some helpful sites.

Aether Madness The full text of a print book about the Net. Lots of information in plain English.
http://www.neo.com/Aether/

c/net on-line Home page of a TV show about the Net; very good features.
http://www.cnet.com/

CyberWire Dispatches Home page of an excellent newsletter about the Net.
http://cyberwerks.com:70/cyberwire/cwd

EFFweb Home page of the Electronic Frontier Foundation, an organization promoting and defending free speech on the Internet.
http://www.eff.org/

Jumbo! The best shareware software archive on the Net, for all types of computers.
http://www.jumbo.com/

THE LIST An excellent directory of Internet service providers, arranged by area code.
http://thelist.internet.com/

NewsHub Constantly updated links to news about the Net available on the Net.
http://www.newshub.com/tech/bytime.html

Point Communications Corporation They pick the "Top 5% Web Sites," an award that is taken very seriously, at least by the chosen sites.
http://www.pointcom.com/

Gleason Sackman's Net-Happenings Home page for the indispensable guide to what's new on the Net.
http://www.mid.net:80/NET/

With Morning Coffee A wake-up page with news, humor, and even links to daily cartoons.
http://www.inkspot.com/admin/coffee.html

USENET NEWSGROUPS

alt.culture.internet

comp.internet.net-happenings

news.answers

rec.answers

Chapter 8

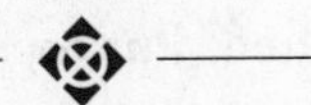

Keeping Up With the Net: How to Stay Abreast of New Resources on the Internet

The newcomer to the Internet often feels like a visitor to a strange new country. There's a new language to be learned, new customs to get used to, and, of course, there's the process of finding your way around. Unfortunately, there's no reliable map of the Internet that you can buy, and even if there were such a map, it would have to be updated nearly every day, for the Internet is growing and changing constantly. Dozens of new sites are launched every day, old favorites change their location or disappear entirely, new Usenet newsgroups are formed, mailing lists are announced, even the software available to roam the Net is being constantly updated.

Fortunately, there are several ways to keep up with developments on the Net. They include mailing lists, Usenet newsgroups, Web pages, e-mail newsletters, and even (gasp!) old-fashioned print-on-paper magazines and books. No single source lists absolutely everything that's new or different on the Net, so most users end up checking several of them every so often. Put together, though, any two or three of these sources will do a pretty good job of keeping you up to date with what's new.

ON-LINE NEWSLETTERS

The Net-Happenings Digest: The easiest way to keep up with the changing landscape of the Net is by subscribing to this e-mail announcement newsletter. It's an especially good way to get news of the Net because it lists new resources of almost all types—Web pages, mailing lists, Net software, other newsletters, and more. *Net-Happenings* is available in several forms: as a digest in newsletter format, as a mailing list of individual announcements, or mirrored as a Usenet newsgroup, **comp.internet.net-happenings**. I recommend that you subscribe to the digest form, because a subscription to the mailing list will fill your in box with dozens of messages every day, and postings to the Usenet newsgroup expire fairly quickly on most news servers so you might easily miss an announcement of interest. The digest form also comes with a handy table of contents in each issue, so you can see right away whether there's anything of interest to you.

To subscribe to the *Net-Happenings Digest*, send an e-mail message to **listserv@lists.internic.net**, leaving the subject line blank and the body of the message reading "subscribe Net-happenings-digest *your full name.*" You can also search the *Net-Happenings* archives, as well as see the most recent issue, at **http://scout.cs.wisc.edu/scout/net-hap.** If you have something to announce, check out the handy submittal form.

Special Internet Connections: Another good newsletter, which can be had by sending an e-mail message to **listserv@csd.uwm.edu**, subject line blank, message reading "subscribe inetlist *your full name.*"

The IWatch Digest: Subscribe by sending an e-mail message to **listserv@garcia.com**, with a blank subject line and "subscribe IWatch *your full name*" in the body.

Seidman's Online Insider: If you're interested in general news about the Net, including technological innovations, censorship, and the evolution of the Net itself, you should subscribe to this newsletter. Send an e-mail message to **listserv@peach.ease.lsoft.com** and in the body of the message type "subscribe online-1 *your full name.*" The *Online Insider* can also be found at **http://www.onlineinsider.com**

Edupage: Describes itself as "a summary of news items on information technology," but it's much more interesting than it sounds. Send requests to **listproc@educom.unc.edu** and in the body of the message type "subscribe edupage *your full name.*" The same folks also produce *The Educom Review*, a "bimonthly print magazine on learning, communications, and information technology," so they pay special attention to learning resources on the Net.

USENET NEWSGROUPS

comp.infosystems.www.announce: The place to find announcements of new resources on the Web, so you'll probably want to set your newsreader to subscribe to this group.

rec.arts.books: Many new sites and resources on the Net are announced in this newsgroup.

news.announce.newgroups: For news about new Usenet newsgroups. Most newsreaders, by the way, have a "get new group" feature of some sort, so it's fairly easy to see what new newsgroups your provider has chosen to carry. There's still a strong case to be made for reading **news.announce.newgroups**, however—if there's a new group that you're interested in reading but your provider has chosen not to pick it up, chances are good that they'll carry it if you ask them nicely.

comp.internet.net-happenings: The *Net-Happenings* newsletter (see above) is reposted to this newsgroup.

THE WEB

The Yahoo! home page (**http://www.yahoo.com**): Another good way to keep up with what's new on the Web is to check here every so often, where you'll find what the Yahoo-sters consider notable new sites on the Web.

There are also a growing number of sites that feature the "Cool Site of the Day" or the like. If you're primarily looking for resources connected to books and reading, however, these sites tend to be a waste of time. The Web pages they pick may be "cool" (especially to those who routinely use the word *cool* in conversation, I suppose), but they are rarely intellectually rewarding.

One overlooked way to find new things on the Net is simply to use the search engines of the Web (see Chapter 3 for a listing). Check under such general categories as "Books" or "Libraries." Most of the results you'll get back will already be familiar to you, but there will almost always be a few new jewels in the mix.

MAGAZINES

Magazines (the print-on-paper kind) devoted to the Internet have multiplied rapidly, as have the number of mainstream computer magazines now offering some coverage of the Internet. In general, magazines aimed specifically at Internet users are far more likely to point you in the right direction than are the general computer magazines, which have proven to be remarkably clueless when it comes to the Net. Unfortunately, Net-specific magazines have proven to have a very short life span over the past few years. Some of the best of the breed (*The Net*, *Virtual City*, and *Internet Underground*) have gone out of business, while other once-worthwhile guides to the Net (*Internet World*, *Net Guide*) have shifted their focus from trying to make sense of the Net for the average user to promoting the greedhead "Internet Gold Rush" mentality with articles along the lines of "How to Make Big Bucks on the Web." These magazines are now worse than useless to anyone who cares about the actual content of the Net, although "cyberspammers" probably find them quite useful.

Two magazines still worth reading are:

The Web—Good site listings and a healthy sense of humor make this magazine a good bet.

Wired—This "journal of the digital age" can be a good source of news about the Net, but it espouses a heady mix of cyberevangelism and consumerism that some people find annoying. I stopped reading *Wired* for a couple of years, but I've started again because they seem to be some of the few folks around who remember what the Internet was supposed to be about.

BOOKS

Because the Internet is growing so rapidly, the various Internet directories that you find in bookstores are almost certainly at least slightly outdated by the time they're published, although the best of them will still contain a great deal of valuable information. One Net directory in particular stands out, however:

Harley Hahn's Internet & Web Yellow Pages (4th ed., Osborne McGraw-Hill 1997, $29.99). Of the several directories calling themselves "Internet Yellow Pages" to be found in bookstores, by far the best is this one, and it comes with the full text of the book itself on an enclosed CD-ROM. Hahn lists resources of all types (Web, Gopher, Usenet, etc.) by subject in a clear and logical format, interspersed with unexpected but welcome bits of humor. This book contains so many neat things that you'll want to log onto the Net immediately after browsing through just a few pages.

Ultimately, your best source of information about new things on the Net is likely to be the Net itself. Remember that simply because you've visited a site once doesn't mean that you've seen it all, and the best sites periodically update themselves with new material and links to other places on the Net.

Index

academic origins, Internet, 5, 12, 12–13, 97–98
mailing lists, 97–98
academic subjects, list of mailing lists, 101
Active X, 60
addresses on Internet (deciphering URL) 123–25
cropping, 125
addresses, mailing lists, 98–99
Adobe Page Mill, 115–16
ads, 9
commercial incursions, 16–17, 60
Agent software, 80
Agent, Forte's, newsreader, 43
All-in-One Search Page (**http://www.albany.net/allinone/**), 55, 127–28
alt. groups (Usenet), 75–76
creating an, 88–90
Altavista (**http://www.altavista.digital.com**), 128
America Online (AOL), 6, 35–42, 121, 145–46, 175, 192, 233, 239–40, 253, 261
ancient and classical literature (indexes), 183–84
ARPANET (Advanced Research Projects Agency) and the U.S. Department of Defense, 4–5
ASCII, 112, 114
text editors, 115

audiences, Web pages, 118–19
authors, on-line, 8
  authors, specific, general
    indexes of, 146–65

baud, 25, 27–28
BBC World Service, xvi
best-sellers, excerpts of on the
    Internet, xvii
book discussion groups, xv–xvi
    on-line, 9–10
book lovers, on-line resources,
    8–12, 39, 120–264
  America Online (AOL), 121,
    145–46
  authors, specific, general
    indexes of, 146–65
  book publishers, 208–10
  book reviews, 210–13
  book stores, 203–7
  dictionaries and other language
    resources, 240–44
  e-text publishers and
    distributors, 210–2
  e-texts, 197–201
  e-zines and literary journals,
    214–28
  FAQ files, 132–145
  forums, 92
  general indexes and
    "Metapages," 126–27
  hypertext literature, 202–3
  indexes (see: indexes)
  lack of on-line services for, 48
  libraries, 245–48
  Liszt of Newsgroups and
    PAML, 122
  magazines on-line, 230–33
  magazines, on-line, 229
  news, other sources, 238–39
  newspapers on-line, 233–34
  newspapers, on-line, 233
  on the Web, 58–59, 121
  reference sources, 248–50
  specialty providers for . . .
    and readers, 46–50
  The WELL, 48–50, 121, 146
  Usenet groups, 122
*Book Lovers: Fine Books and
    Literature* (**http://www.
    xs4all.nl/~pwessel/**), 10
book sellers on-line, xvii
books (to stay current with the
    Net), 270–71
books on the Internet, 18–20
browsers, 8, 43–44, 54–56
  formatting codes, 55
  image maps, 55
  Microsoft, 55, 80
  Netscape, 43, 54–55, 80
  secure transmission forms, 55
bulletin boards, book
    discussions, xvi
  Web-based, 70–71

censorship, 5, 12
chat rooms, 66–68
  channels, 68
  downside, 67–68
  real time, 71
children's books & reading
    resources on the
    Internet, 165–68
ClariNet, 76–77
Compuserve, 6, 35–40
Computer Shopper, 34

computers, for accessing Internet, 22–25
graphic interface, 24
host, 124
obsolete, 23–24
old and text-based, 24
RAM, 24
servers, 53
computers, home, boom in, 5
conferencing
members only, 48–49
Salon and *Cafe Utne*, 60
smaller systems, 49–50
time-shifted, 70
Web-based, 70–71, 91–94
content, crisis of, 16
"Cool Site of the Day", 119, 269
cultural studies and multicultural literature, 168–70
culture of the Internet
communalism, 14–15
freedom of speech, 13
netiquette, 13–15
flaming, 14, 73
spamming, 14

DaSilva, Stephanie, 100
Deja News (**http://www.dejanews.com**), 87
for non-Web sites, 55
democratic effect of Internet, xviii, 12, 22–23
Department of Defense (ARPANET), 4–5
diaries and collective writing projects, 260–61
dictionaries and other language resources, on-line, 240–44
"Digital Convergence," 30–31, 47
Directory of Scholarly Electronic Conferences, 101
discussion groups
Internet, on the, 9–12
list of, 93–94
New York Times Book Review, xvi
Usenet, 11–12, 17
Web-based, 91–94
downloading, 62–65

e-mail, 43–44
mailing lists, 95–96
programs (Eudora), 109–10
e-text publishers and distributors, commercial, 201–2
e-texts, 197–201
e-zines and on-line journals, xvi, 107–8, 214–28
indexes of, 213
Echo, 49–50
female users, 50
Ecunet, 48
18th Century and Romantic Literature (indexes), 186
Electronic Newsstand, The, (**http://www.enews.com/**), 9
equipment to use Internet, 23–32
baud, 25
computers, 24–25

equipment to use Internet (*cont'd*)
  do's and don'ts, 25
  DOS, 25
  keyboard, wireless, for Web-TV, 31
  modems, 27–29
  software, 26
  telephone lines, 29–30
"Error 404" (message and e-zine), 125
Eudora, Qualcom's (e-mail), 43, 104–110
Excite Netsearch (**http://www.excite.com**), 128

FAQ (frequently asked questions), 77–78
  book lovers, for, 132–145
fiction, collaborative, 11, 59–60
files, software, 62–65
  "pub" directories, 64
flaming, 14, 73
formatting codes, 55
forums on the Web, 70–71
  Usenet, 70–91
freeware, 35, 67
FTP (File Transfer Protocol) 62–65, 121
  as shareware, 63
  caveats, 64–65
  for uploading, 117
  transfers, 63–64
  unattended sites, 69

gay, lesbian and bisexual literature, indexes of, 170–171
geography, negation of, xvii
Gopher, xvii
government, U.S., information re:, on-line, 250–51
Gutenberg, (see: Project Gutenberg)

home pages, personal, 52, 63
hooking up ("getting wired") to the Internet, 21–50
  "jacking into the Net," 22
  universities, 21
  UNIX, 21–22
horror fiction resources (indexes), 190
horror, science fiction, & fantasy writer's resources, 190–92
host computer, 124
Hotbot (**http://www.hotbot.com**) 128
humor, indexes, 171–73
hypertext markup language (HTML), 112–16, 116
  ASCII and, 112
  ASCII text editors, 115
  authoring tools, 115
  guides, 114
  introductory (free) on Yahoo!, 114–15
  Jumbo Shareware Archives, 115
  learning, 113–14
  Microsoft Word and Word Perfect, 114–15
  saving, 114
  "tags" (formatting codes), 112–13

view source," or "view HTML," 114
Web pages, creating without learning, 116
"WYSIWYG" programs, 115–16
hypertext transfer protocol (HTTP), 53
hypertext, 52–53
literature, 202–3

image maps, 55
indexes
ancient and classical literature, 183–84
authors, specific, 146–65
children's books and reading resources, 165–68
cultural studies, multicultural literature, 168–70
18th Century and Romantic literature, 186
gay, lesbian and bisexual literature, 170–71
horror fiction resources, 190
horror, sci-fi & fantasy writers, resources, 190–92
humor, 171–73
medieval literature, 184–85
modern literature, 187
mystery literature, 173–75
mythology and folklore, 181–83
poetry resources, 175–78
Renaissance literature, 185–86
resources, 129–32
romance writing, 179–89
scholarly literary resources, 180–81
science fiction and fantasy resources, 188–89
theater resources, 192–94
Victorian literature, 186–87
women's literature resources, 194–96
Infoseek Homepage (**http://www.infoseek.com/Home**), 128

Internet
access without a computer, 30–32
academic origins, 5, 12, 12–13, 97–98
anarchic nature of, 13
book discussion groups, xv–xvi
books and the, 18–20
bulletin boards, xvi
censorship, 5
critics, 18–19
culture, 12–15
defined, 2–4
democracy and the, xviii, 12, 22–23
equipment needed to use the, 22–23
e-zines and on-line journals, newspapers, TV news, print magazines, books, xvi–xvii
free access to, 32–33
BBSs (bulletin board systems), 34
free page space, 117
government institutions, 34

Internet (*cont'd*)
institutions, 32
libraries, 34
local area networks (LANs), 33
outside the U.S., Canada, and Europe, 33
university grads, 33–34
geography, negation of/ democratic nature of the, xviii
glacial pace of, 67
growth of, xiii–xiv, 5–6, 52
growing pains, 15–18
crisis of content, 16
porno 16
history, 4–6, 12, 13
hooking up and software requirements, xv, 21–50
"Internet years", xiv
information about, sources of, 262–64
ISPs (Internet service providers), 26
language of, 5
library, limitless, 7–8
life dimension, new, xiv
names and places, understanding, 123–25
networks, 3–4
on-line services, 6, 26, 35–42
projections, future of, 4, 20
organization of, 2
readership, potential, 105
redundancy, 5
resources, keeping up with the newest, 265–71
books, 270–71
e-mail newsletters, 265, 266–67
magazines, 269–70
mailing lists, 265
Web, the—Yahoo!, et al, 268–69
resources for book lovers
Clearinghouse for Subject-Oriented Research Guides, 126
Daedalus's Guides to the Web . . . , 126
Directory of Scholarly Electronic Conferences, 101
indexes, general, and "Metapages," 126–27
Look Smart, 127
Meta-Index of WWW and Internet Resources (NCSA), 127
Meta-Index of WWW Resources, Library of Congress, 127
New Riders' Official World-Wide Web Yellow Pages, 127
Yahoo!, 126
self-sufficiency, xviii
size (and growth of), xiv, 105
text, 6, 7
TV, versus "cutting edge technology" of, 7
use of, statistics re:, 4
Web-TV (**http://www.webtv.com/**), xv, 31–32
Interport, 50
IRC (Internet relay chat), 43, 66–68

ISDN (Integrated Services Digital Network), 30, 50
ISPs (Internet service providers), 43–46
advantages, 43–44
alt. groups, information from, 45
drawbacks, 44–45
independent, 43–46
internal newsgroups, 77
List, The (**http://www.thelist.com**), 45–46
national ISPs, 46
newsfeeds from independents, 76

Java, 60, 67
Talk City and Pathfinder Chat, 67
journalism resources, 256–57
Jumbo Shareware Archives, (**http://www.jumbo.com**), 115

"kill files," 74
"killer apps," 55
Kovacs, Diane (Kent State University) 101

Leeper, Evelyn, 11
LeMay, Laura (*Teach Yourself Web Publishing with HTML in 14 Days*, 113–14
libraries on-line, 245–48
links, 10, 52–53, 54, 56, 57, 87
checking, 117
options, 58
personal Web pages, on, 112
Web rings, 60–61
listservers, 98–99, 100, 110–11
Liszt of Lists, Search the (**http://catalog.com/vivian/interest-group-search.html**), 100
Liszt of Lists, The (**http://www.liszt.com**), 86–87, 122
literary resources, scholarly (indexes), 180–81
Lycos Home Page (**http://www.lycos.com/**), 128

magazines, print, on the Internet, xvi–xvii
computer, 25
Electronic Newsstand, The, 9
index of, 229
on-line editions, 9, 230–233
staying current via, 265
Web-based, with book discussion groups, 10
Magellan (**http://www.mckinley.com/**), 128
mailing lists, 95–104
academic origins, 97
announcements of new lists, 101–2
benefits, 97
blind carbon copy" (BBC), 110
community, 97
directories and indexes, 100–1
Directory of Scholarly Electronic Conferences, 101

mailing lists (*cont'd*)
Net-Happenings, 101
Nova Southeastern U. E-mail Discussion Group, 100–01
Publicly Accessible Mailing Lists (PAML), 100
Search the Liszt of Lists, 100
e-mail (Eudora), 109–10
ease of use, 96–97
finding, 99–102
growth of, 96
on-line, 9
publicly accessible, 55
staying current via, 265
subject, by, 55
subscribing to, 98–99
volume, 104
without Internet access, 96
Majordomo, 101, 110, 122
medieval literature (indexes), 184–85
Microsoft Front Page, 115–16
Microsoft Internet Explorer, 55, 93
Microsoft Network (MSN), 35
Microsoft Word, 114–15
modems, 27–29
brands, 29
external, 27
speed, 27–28
upgrades, 28
modern literature (indexes), 187
Mosaic Web browser, 43, 54
revolutionizing the Web, 55
MSNBC, xvi, 62
multipart binary files, 41
mystery literature (indexes), 173–75
mythology and folklore (indexes), 181–83

names (and places) on the Internet, understanding, 123–25
NCSA (National Center for Supercomputing Applications), 54
Net-Happenings, (**http://www.mid.net**), 101, 109, 266–67
"Net kooks," 13, 74, 103
"Net potatoes," 70
"net" prefix, 91
netiquette, 13–15, 73–74, 77–78, 103
Netscape, 43, 54–55, 87, 93
networks, 3–4
New York Times Book Review (discussion groups & bulletin boards), xvi
Round Table Forum, 93
"newbies," 12, 16, 31
news delivery services, personal, 47–48
broad-based, 47–48
news, other sources of on the Internet, 238–39
news, TV, on the Internet, xvi
newsgroups
information, finding, about, 86–87
Liszt of Newsgroups, The, 86–87
local, 76–77
moderated, 77
readers, for, 81–86

starting one on Usenet, 87–90
Usenet, 41, 55, 68, 70, 71–78, 122
newspapers on the Internet, xvi
daily digital, 47
indexes of, 233–34
New York Times Book Review, The, 234–37
newsreaders, 43
Usenet, 78–81
subscribing, 78
software, 79
shareware, 80
off-line capability, 80–81
Nova Southeastern University E-Mail Discussion Group, 100–1
newsletters, starting, 108–11
length, 109
updates via, 266–67
Yahoo!, 108

on-line services, 35–40
appeal of, 39–40, 41
central control, 36
e-mail software, 110
free software, 35
growth of, 5–6
kingdoms unto themselves, 35–36
newsreaders, drawbacks of, 79
on-line service features, 36–39
chat rooms, 36
native content, 37
problems, 38–39
trial accounts, 37–38
Usenet, 36
Web browsers, 36
slowness of connections, 44
Web page creation, 116
organizations, writers', 259

packets of data (TCP/IP), 5
page, 53
parents, concerns of, 40–42
Peace Net, 47
penpals, 95–96
soc.penpals (Usenet), 96
personal Web pages
audiences for, 118–19
construction tools, 114–17
crisis of content, 16
on-line services, 116
pitfalls in creating, 117–18
updating, 119
uploading, 117
without learning HTML, 116
poetry resources (indexes), 175–78
pornography, 16, 40–42
postings, 87
print publications, on-line versions, 10–11, 58, 108
Prodigy, 6
profits from Internet business, xvii
Project Gutenberg (**http://www.promo.net/pg/**), 8, 106
e-texts at, 198
goals, 8
public domain (free), 8

publications on-line, 10–11
university role in, 11
Publicly Accessible Mailing Lists, (PAML), 100–2
publishers, on-line, 208–10
publishing, self-, 105–19
advantages and disadvantages, 106–7
Internet readership, 105
Usenet, 106–7
"push" technology, 61–62

rec.art.books, 11–12
FAQs, 11
Leeper, Evelyn, 11
redundancy, 5
reference (other) resources on-line, 251–53
reference sources on-line, 248–50
Renaissance literature (indexes), 185–86
romance writing (indexes), 179–80
"rtfm," 77–78

Sackman, Gleason, 101
Salon (bulletin boards and discussion groups) (**http://www.salon1999.com**), 10, 60, 94
SavvySearch (**http://www.cs.colostate.edu/~dreiling/smartform.html**), 128
science fiction and fantasy resources (indexes), 188–89
screenwriting, 259–60
"search" button, 57
search engines, 56–58, 127–28
books and libraries, 269
Yahoo!, 48, 57, 128
All-in-One Search Page, 55, 127–28
Altavista, 128
Excite Netsearch, 128
Hotbot, 128
Infoseek Home Page, 128
Lycos Home Page, 128
Magellan, 128
SavvySearch, 128
WebCrawler Searching, 128
secure transmission forms, 55
self-publishing, 105–119
advantages and disadvantages, 106–7
Internet readership, 105
Usenet, 106–7
self-sufficiency on the Internet, xviii
serial-line Internet protocol (SLIP)/point-to-point protocol (PPP), 43, 45, 50, 63, 79–80
server, 53
shareware, 26, 80
Jumbo, 115
signal-to-noise ratio, 15
software for the Internet, 26
ISPs, 43–46
on-line services, 26, 35, 36, 37, 38
"suite" or "Swiss Army Knife" (Agent), 80
spam, 14, 17, 73, 90–91

subscribers (newsletter) as
resources, 111
"surfing," 69

"tags" (HTML formatting
codes), 112–13
Teach Yourself Web Publishing Without HTML in 14 Days, 113
telephone lines for accessing the
Internet, 29–30
ISDNs and new networks, 30
second line, 29
T1 or T3 data connections,
30, 45
telephone company, 29
telnet, 50, 65–66, 121
library catalogs, 66
on-line services, via, 65
text, as the essence of the
Internet, 6, 7
text-based systems, 24, 79
theater resources (indexes),
192–94
threads, 72
time shifted, 70
transmission control protocol/
Internet protocol
(TCP), 5, 79–80
TV news on the Internet, xvi

uniform resource locator
(URL), 123–25
universities, 5, 12, 12–13, 21,
32–33, 97–98, 111
writing programs, 256
UNIX, 21–22
"gurus" or "wizards," 21
interface, 55
newsreaders, 79
Up to the Minute News (CBS)
on the Internet, xvi
uploading Web pages, 117
Usenet
alt. groups, 75–76
alt. groups, starting, 75–76
book lover resources, 122
caveat, 86
discussion groups, 11–12
downside, 90–91
growth, 73
hierarchy, 76
history, 72
information, finding, 86–87
names of, other, 78
Net updates via, 266–67
netiquette, 73–74
new mailing lists, list of, 101
newsgroups for readers,
81–86
newsgroups, 41, 55, 68, 70,
71–74, 122, 268
newsreaders, 78–81
opinions, 72
organization of, 74–78
family tree, 75
hierarchy, 74–76
official and unofficial
groups, 75–76
penalties, 74
self-publishing on, 106–7
starting a, 87–90
variety of groups, 17
Utne Reader Cafe Utne (**http://www.utne.com/**), 10,
60, 93

Victorian literature (indexes), 186–87
"view HTML" or "view source," 114

WebCrawler Searching (**http://www.webcrawler.com/**), 128
Websites
  audiences for, 118–19
  construction tools, 114–17
  creating without learning HTML, 116
  creating, 112–13
  on-line services, 116
  personal pages, 16, 53
  personal publishing on, 111–12
  pitfalls in creating, 117–18
  proliferation, 2–3
  total, growth in, 56, 120
  unattended, 69
  updating, 119
  uploading, 117
writing, experiments in, 11
written word, future of, xviii
Wesselmen, Piet, 10
Web Wizard (**http://www.halcyon.com/artamedia/webwizard/**), 116
WELL, The, 48–50, 121, 146, 175, 192, 194, 228, 261–62
Washington Post Book World, The (BBs & discussion groups), xvi
WordPerfect, 114–15
women's literary resources (indexes), 194–96
"WYSIWYG" (what you see is what you get) programs, 115–16
World Wide Web, 16, 51
  collection of documents, as, 53
  discussion groups, list of, 93–94
  forums, 70–71, 91–94
  growth of, 120
  invention of, 52
  Mosaic, 54
Web-TV (**http://www.webtv.com/**), xv, 23, 47
Web rings, 60–61
  directory (**http://www.webring.org/ringworld**), 61
writing resources, 253–62
  diaries and collective writing projects, 260–61
  general resources, 254–56
  helpful resources for writers, 257–59
  journalism resources, 256–57
  screenwriting, 259–60
  university writing programs and laboratories, 256
  writers' organizations, 259

Yahoo! (**http://www.yahoo.com**), 48, 57, 80, 108, 114, 115, 128, 268

About the Author

Evan Morris's column on words and language, *The Word Detective*, appears in newspapers in the United States, Mexico, and Japan (and is available on the World Wide Web at **http://www.word-detective.com**). He also writes a weekly column on slang for *The New York Daily News.* Mr. Morris has years of experience on both the Internet and on-line services and the phone bills to prove it. He is married, has one son, and lives in New York City.

